T0245607

I'm a big fan of anyone generous enough to outline the steps we need to take to implement great changes. Adam gives more than clear practical steps but also an insight into his brilliant framework. An irreverent, straight-talking and clever book to get you taking those steps to being outside the matrix 9–5.

Lucy Werner, Author & Founder of hypeyourself.com

This book has EVERYTHING you want to think about if you're ready to 'make the leap'. The future is bright, and super rewarding, I've done it! But setting yourself up for success is the most important part and this book has totally got you covered.

Tom Coleman, Social Media & Marketing Expert & Corporate Escapologist

So, you're thinking of leaving your corporate job? But you're not sure if you can do it, let alone how to do it. If this is you, then here is your go-to book that I'll be putting into the hands of every person wanting to take that leap into the unknown. It's a practical, thorough approach to thinking through this change – even if you decide to stay. Once you have worked through Adam's step-by-step approach, you'll have increased your confidence, your self-worth and definitely understood your value to the marketplace. Highly recommended!

Dr Lucy Ryan, author, 'Revolting Women: Why midlife women are walking out (and what to do about it)'

People with corporate experience make excellent board advisors, they bring a wealth of knowledge and expertise. A proactive and planned transition from a corporate career, as advocated in this book, helps people get ready for what's next and start adding value earlier.

Louise Broekman, CEO Advisory Board Centre

If you want to be somewhere other than your corporate job this time next year, you need this book.

Kia Cannons, Artist, Coach & Corporate Escapologist

Corporate Escapology

A practical guide to **breaking free** and **moving on**

ADAM FORBES

First published in Great Britain by Practical Inspiration Publishing, 2024

ISBN   9781788606028 (hardback)
        9781788606035 (paperback)
        9781788606059 (epub)
        9781788606042 (mobi)

Want to bulk-buy copies of this book for your team and colleagues? We can customize the content and co-brand *Corporate Escapology* to suit your business's needs.

Please email info@practicalinspiration.com for more details.

Practical Inspiration
Publishing

To my first believer, my mum, Andy Forbes, who spent her whole life in libraries and would have been very proud her son had his own ISBN.

Contents

List of exercises

Foreword
Claire Perry-Louise

Sometimes you just have to take the leap.

Sometimes you leapt and you didn't realise you were leaping.

Sometimes fear stops you leaping but that fear keeps you stuck.

We are born into our unique realities. We learn from our caretakers what is and isn't right. How we should and shouldn't be in the world, what is success and what isn't.

Does this make any of it right or wrong? No. I have no judgement on the belief systems you operate from. They have come from your very own life experience and you are entitled to them.

Those who raise us are often unconsciously imposing their own belief systems on to us because they make sense to them. Generations see the world through very different social, economic and political standpoints.

My dad grew up in a society where being a solicitor was an indicator of security and success. It created all of the things he valued in the world and he wanted the best for me. I wanted to be a hairdresser or work in hotel management but he dismissed these and said, 'Claire, you can come back to that, start with law, you can go anywhere with that.'

In 2004, I qualified as a solicitor.

A career that did not fill my heart with joy. Yet I had ticked the boxes.

I managed to play the game. I did my time in the law firms and I guess I still would be there if fate hadn't played a hand.

In 2011, I came across a YouTube video, presented by an entrepreneur who had made millions online.

I watched the clip and I immediately decided I wanted to attend the three-day course he had created, sharing his strategies and approach.

This was the catalyst. My life was about to swiftly change direction.

I didn't know what I was doing but I knew I was excited about learning something new. I was excited to explore a world I had never been in before. I set off at great pace. Diving deep into personal development and uncovering who 'Claire' actually was.

Claire had forgotten. She only knew who she was supposed to be.

She only knew to be the good girl. To get the grades. To get the husband and buy the house.

Until the day she realised there was more inside of her.

Spring forward to 2024, I'm still figuring out who I am. Turns out all the conditioning and limiting beliefs from the past don't just go away all by themselves.

Yet I do know this.

I am fuelled by passion and purpose. I've made a difference. I've built a community called the Like Hearted Leaders. It's for fellow trailblazers, figuring out how to run a business alone and deal with some of the inconveniences of being human.

My story is my own.

You will have your own unique story to navigate.

Yet, let me leave you with this:

We are here to explore the entirety of the human experience. We can sail along on the good times. Clinging to the safety we pretend is real. Maintaining the status quo so we don't upset those around us.

However, this is the truth of it.

You are a one of a kind. Inside you is so much more.

Growth comes not from the smooth sailing but from the rough seas and storms you will weather.

Adam has written this book to help you see the real you, distinct from your corporate identity, rich with experience and skills and bursting with potential. He shows us how to prepare for an exciting new chapter of our lives, one filled with purpose, optimism and grounded self-confidence.

Corporate Escapology is a second chance for all of us who have spent years being who we were supposed to be but are now waking up to who we are and can be. You won't just find inspiration here, but a practical and motivational Escape Plan for making the shift that will change your life forever.

Believe in yourself.

Love yourself.

You've got this.

Big love,

Claire

Founder of Like Hearted Leaders & Community Architect

Introduction

When I was 14 our class had a careers lesson. We'd never had one before. I remember being quite excited, looking into the future, my future. We were given some strange forms and had to answer questions about our strengths and weaknesses, likes and dislikes. The form was fed into a machine called a computer, which would deliver our fate (weeks later, it was 1988).

I was on tenterhooks.

Until I saw what early artificial intelligence had in mind for me: Accountant, Retail Manager, Bank Manager. But one option in particular made my heart sink: Office Worker.

The computer spat out more vocational options for my classmates: Florist, Plumber, Lawyer, Doctor.

I remember not telling my parents.

I felt like I needed to bury any hint of predetermination.

And yet, an Office Worker is what I became. The computer was right.

I spent most of my early career working in offices. For pretty big companies. Who had, thankfully, become a bit more creative with the job titles.

And I loved it.

It played to many of my strengths, allowing me to work on big things that mattered, with bright, capable people. It let me travel, provided a steady, stable income while my children were young – and for the most part, it was actually pretty good fun.

Until it wasn't.

It was never truly awful. I didn't feel nauseous going into work or dread Sunday nights (as many people do). I just became a bit bored. I coasted unfulfilled. And later on, when I reflected, I think I was disappointed. Partly in the corporate for whom I worked, but mostly in myself.

I knew I was capable of more. I knew I wasn't growing and I wasn't progressing as fast as I had done earlier on. In truth, I had settled for an easy, comfortable and safe life.

And it didn't feel good.

Settling rarely does.

So, when the next wave of restructuring appeared on the horizon (I didn't need to wait long), I put my hand up to leave.

I was fortunate, I had time to adjust to a life outside. But with three children under 13, and little experience of 'life on the outside', it felt like a bold move.

Several years on, as I write this, it doesn't feel nearly so bold. Or even that much of a risk.

Still, it's the best thing I ever did career-wise – and life-wise.

Moreover, what followed next could <u>only</u> have happened because of 20 years working in – and with – corporates.

I started writing a blog called Corporate Escapologist the first month I left my job and set out on a journey to find out what I'd do next.

Through the blog I met hundreds of people, just like me, who had left their corporate jobs. We were in mixed emotional states – a spectrum of anxiety: from mild (mostly excited) to intense (crippled by rejection, and in some cases complete shock). People told me the blog helped; they said it was like 'someone was inside their head', describing the range of feelings they were going through.

During the years since I left my corporate career, I've tried many things – Startup founder, Consultant, Mentor, Expert

Advisor, Blogger, Trainer, Workshopper, Programme director, Coach and now Author.

Most of these roles have involved working closely with corporates in some way or another. I'm fascinated by them, how they work and the points of intersection they have with other businesses, governments, startups, non-government organizations (NGOs) and the general public.

And I'm especially fascinated by the people who work for corporates.

Because I see myself in them.

Over the decades working in corporate life, I've talked to thousands of people who, like me, settled into a career that no longer served them. Many confided in me about wanting to leave, wanting to do something more purposeful, wanting to set up their own business, wanting to go it alone, wanting more time for life outside, wanting more variety, more control, more autonomy.

But, despite the urges, despite the frustrations, most never left.

Most never will.

Because they feel like there's too much at stake.

It's taken years, maybe decades, to build a career and now people are depending on them – and the money they bring home.

It's no wonder they're a bit scared.

But it's not a way to live life – in fear.

That's where I'm hoping *Corporate Escapology* can help: it's a practical guide to breaking free of corporate life and moving on.

It's about getting prepared.

And then it's about seeing it through.

The Escape Method and Escape Plan Canvas

During my research for this book, I interviewed over a hundred people who had left corporate jobs to build new lives for themselves.

Three things stood out above all else:

1   Every single person said they were happy they had left
    their corporate career and were now enjoying their work
    more – and their life more.

2   Every single person recognized that their corporate career
    was formative in helping them to be successful today.

3   Every single person, quite unconsciously, followed a similar
    path before, during and after their exit from corporate life.

I call this path the Escape Method: five stages to get ready to
leave and land safely. The first four will decouple you from
corporate life and help you build a new one in its place, the
fifth will help you sustain that life.

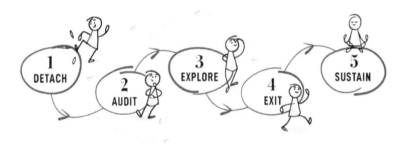

Each stage of the Escape Method is covered in a separate part
of the book:

o   Part I helps you Detach, shifting your mindset to really
    see corporates for what they are (the good, the bad and
    the ugly) and helps move you to a more positive, more
    confident state.

o   Part II helps you Audit the skills, experiences and
    know-how that make you distinctive and valuable in the
    outside world. It will also help you become clearer about
    your boundaries, constraints and goals.

o   Part III helps you to Explore, gathering inspiration from
    different opportunities and pathways. I'll introduce you to
    other people who have made the leap to something new, so
    that you can see what's worked for them and what might
    be possible for you.

o   Part IV helps you Exit the job and land safely – with a new identity, new networks and new capabilities. It's here where you will really test what's holding you back – and where you will execute your escape.

o   Part V helps you Sustain your new life, dealing with the wobbles, the things that don't go to plan and how to bounce back.

The Escape Method may look like a linear approach to breaking free and moving on. But life doesn't work like this.

It's more iterative, with moments of pause, reflection and self-doubt as well as spurts of growth as your capacity for change increases and you begin to see what's possible.

My single mission with this book is to help build your self-confidence, self-belief and self-worth, whether that results in exiting your corporate job or not. If you choose to stay, but with intention, with more self-confidence and without fear, then this book will have done its job.

A file inside a cake

I have developed a set of tools to help you break free and land safely and successfully on the other side. Like a file inside a cake to help you cut through the bars of your corporate job.

They're actually more useful to help progress your thinking as you manage your exit, to cover all the bases and reduce the risk of failing.

One of these tools is the Escape Plan Canvas, a place where you can jot down your ideas and reflections as you work through the Escape Method. At various stages throughout the book, I'll remind you about the Canvas (it appears here in the Introduction, but there is also a double page version in the Appendix). I recommend that you transpose your thoughts, ideas and questions here, so you can keep an ongoing record for later.

Escape Plan Canvas

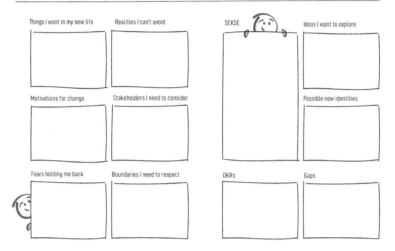

A few elements might look strange right now – SEKSE and OKRs, for instance – but stick with me, we'll get there over the coming pages.

Leaving your corporate job may take time. Years even. Because there's such a lot at stake.

Every year or so, I thought very seriously about leaving my job. I'd buy myself a new notebook and fill it with ideas and plans – then I'd get distracted with work and forget everything. This book has been designed so you can start and stop your escape planning and come back to it later, picking up from where you left off.

It's for yoo-hoo

It might be Confirmation Bias (when you only look for evidence that reinforces your beliefs), but I only get one of three responses when I tell people I'm writing a book about how to leave corporate life:

A 'Hurry up, I need it now'.

B 'I wish you'd written it a few months/years back – I could have done with it then'.

C   'Hurry up, I know someone who needs it now'.

Unhappiness at work is sadly all too common. The statistics bear this out, with engagement at an all-time low and more than half of people planning to be in a different job this time next year[1].

Making people happy is hard. There aren't quick fixes, the sheep-dip solutions don't work. We're all different.

When I started writing this book I wondered if I should do some primary research into why we aren't happier at work. I suspect it was prevarication on my part to avoid getting on with the writing. But I also realized there was enough excellent material out there on why things aren't working (see the Further reading section at the end of the book).

What we need, instead of more research, is something practical, a guide, a way to become happier in our work and in our lives. And since my experience is leaving corporate life and building a life that serves me better, giving me the income I need and rebuilding my confidence, I thought that's what I'd write: a practical guide to breaking free and moving on.

Many people I coach are trading happiness today for blind faith in their future happiness. They don't enjoy their job but feel it's a necessary precondition for a better future (promotion, salary, bonus). Some are considering staying 20 years in a job just to get the pension. Others see only a limited view of themselves and don't believe they can do more.

I wrote this book because I want to help people, like you, feel more confident and happier today. And I want to help you deliver on your potential and your ambitions for the future.

I want to help you enjoy this one shot we all have at life.

Writing in books

Some people see writing in books as sacrilege. Some just see it as a waste – stopping you from passing it on or sending it to the charity shop. I never write in books.

---

[1] Gallup's State of the Global Workplace, 2023.

So, it's hypocritical of me to tell <u>you</u> to write in this book. But I really want you to. This book is practical and whilst you don't have to write in every section, you'll miss an opportunity to clarify your thinking, jot down ideas you'll otherwise forget and build the foundations of your offer to the world for after you have left corporate life.

I can't count the number of self-help books I've bought over the years, whose brilliance was utterly wasted on me because I didn't write things down as I read them. I've tried to make it really easy here, low pressure, simple structures – just to provide a place for your thoughts.

And because I know some people just really, really hate writing in books, send me a photo of your annotated book to @corporateescapologist on Instagram or on LinkedIn and I'll post you a pristine copy you can give to a friend or to the charity shop.

That's how much I want you to really *use* this book, not just *read* it.

But if you really can't face writing in books, visit corporateescapology.com/tools for all the exercise templates in this book.

Now let's get started, we've got a lot of work to do.

I Detach from your corporate career

Leaving your corporate career takes bravery. It's never an easy decision. Because you've worked hard for it. And you're probably quite dependent on it.

Walking away from it sounds like career suicide.

Without a plan it might be.

Part I is the foundation of your Escape Plan: beginning by learning how to detach yourself both from your corporate career and from some of the unhelpful thinking that holds you back.

In Chapter 1, I'm going to help you face up to some of the realities of the corporate experience. Then you'll move to look outside your corporate confines in Chapter 2 to explore what has changed in the work environment over the past decade or two. Chapter 3 is about myth-busting and unloading some of the baggage you may carry. You'll end this first section of the book by projecting forward and learning to 'stand on the veranda' in Chapter 4, looking back at what you're leaving behind – and beginning to get comfortable with it.

CHAPTER 1

Life in a corporate

'There are 32 ways to write a story, and I've used every one, but there is only one plot – things are not as they seem'.

Jim Thompson, Writer

What is a corporate?

The correct term is 'Corporation' and it's defined by Investopedia as 'a legal entity that is separate and distinct from its owners'.

And that's an interesting place to start, because by being distinct from its owners, a corporate is distinct from the human beings who own and/or run it. A corporate is an organizational construct set up to do something, usually to make lots of money.

Corporates tend to be big, like the huge multi-national brands Coca-Cola, Unilever and Ford and, increasingly now, the Big Tech firms, like Apple, Google and Meta.

But corporate is an adjective as well as a noun. Many, much smaller companies feel just as corporate as the huge multi-nationals: they're formal, hierarchical, powerful, functionalized, etc.

If you're in a reasonable sized company and you're wondering if you could do something different with the skills, experience and know-how you've amassed, then this book is for you.

The good things about corporates

I remember the pride I felt receiving the job offer. Even if it was a somewhat sterile PDF over email. I cherished the logo at the top of the page, the words that said, 'We want you', the fancy job title, the dazzling salary and rockstar benefits. I'd come from a small boutique strategy consultancy, run by its owner, with great clients, but definitely no corporate frills.

There's no denying the kudos of working for a big company – and the many, many benefits: scale, impact, (relative) stability, maybe it's multi-national and you'll get to travel. Maybe it's a name your parents (or even your children) know. The salary might be pretty decent too, with an annual bonus, share options, generous holiday, medical insurance, the list goes on and on. Your partner might even benefit if you die in service. It can feel very reassuring.

What's more, corporates are changing: there's a new emphasis on employee well-being as well as a much-needed focus on diversity, equity and inclusion (although it's not universal). In good times, there's fruit on the desks, subsidized lunches, awaydays in stately homes and lavish Christmas parties with ice sculptures.

I loved it. Who wouldn't? With three small children and a hefty mortgage, working for a corporate was a dream come true.

The less good things about corporates

'Dream come true' may be pushing it. I had to deal with many things I didn't really enjoy: pointless meetings, power politics, large egos, futile processes, the endless switching between feast and famine (often in the same year) – and a general acceptance of 'quite average'.

I could put up with most of the things I didn't enjoy when these were weighed against the benefits. Sometimes, the balance even felt tipped in my favour.

'Are you crazy?' I thought, every time I started to peek over the precipice and wonder what life outside might look like.

But increasingly I began having those thoughts more often.

Every few months I would start thinking about leaving, usually to start my own business. I wasn't attracted by working for another corporate; I think I knew they'd all be the same – and maybe this one was rather good.

But at some stage every year I would more than day dream: I would buy a domain name, build a website, set up a side-hustle.

When my second child was born, I was doing a job I really didn't enjoy. I had this brilliant idea of a subscription business, selling a box of locally sourced food and drink. Years before Hello Fresh or Gousto there was eatlocale, which I was planning to franchise (probably globally). After one really annoying day in the office, I came home to tell my wife, Megan, that I was jacking in the well-paid corporate job to build eatlocale.

It was an abject lesson in poor stakeholder management; it made us both miserable.

I even told my boss I wanted out. Luckily, she talked me down from the ledge and helped me find a job in which both she, and my wife, hoped I'd be happier.

And I was for a bit.

That's another good thing about corporates I forgot to mention: you've got options inside the company – you can move about.

Corporates are great.

Aren't they?

Nothing is perfect and a corporate career is no different. It can be exciting and fulfilling. It can be dull and routine. It can be hard work and overwhelming. It can be toxic and destructive. Sometimes all at the same time.

Four confounding things about corporates:

1   Change

In one sense it can feel like nothing ever changes, the monthly, quarterly, annual cycles, same old, same old.

And yet at the same time, it can also feel like the company is in a constant state of flux, where one reorganization bleeds into another, with new systems, new processes, new employee engagement programmes. And where everyone seems to be waiting for something to happen.

Change fatigue is a very real problem in many corporates.

2   Ageism

Ageism is driving many people, particularly women, out of the workforce. It's not legal of course and it's quite challenging to prove, but the gradual passing over of eminently qualified candidates because they don't 'fit' is well-documented.

Dr Lucy Ryan's illuminating book 'Revolting Women' demands that C-Suites wake up to the fact that women are leaving the workforce in droves. Her research suggests as many as 70% don't particularly want to leave, but they do because of what she calls a series of 'collisions' that hit women in the 'midlife smashup': menopause, parental care and loss, children stressing with exams and the proverbial 'empty nest'.

And just when they are wrestling with all that, they're passed over for promotions, career-enhancing opportunities or frankly any interesting work because they're 'getting on a bit'.

The personal accounts in Lucy's book make you want to weep. And the loss of talent and expertise should make every shareholder in a corporate start asking questions.

And whilst this ageism has an irrefutable gender bias, there are the diminishing career prospects for men too, faced with a cult of the 'young leader' who may appeal to younger stakeholders but lack experience and wisdom.

3   Care

Corporates can fool you into believing they care – and that they feel an emotional connection with their employees. Programmes that cultivate shared purpose and values humanize the organization to drive commitment and loyalty.

The recent trend towards employee well-being is grounded in economic logic rather than paternalistic care.

This may not be as sinister as it sounds. In fact, employees may well have just got the wrong end of the stick and started believing in something rather old-fashioned, called the Benevolent Employer (which may never really have existed).

But this can be confusing for an employee. Especially if the company doesn't behave as expected.

Like the Philip Larkin poem about your mum and dad, corporates 'f*** you up, they may not mean to, but they do'.

4   Confidence

This is the big problem I have observed in working with thousands of utterly brilliant people, like you, in corporate jobs: your confidence can erode over time. But why? I think there are three big reasons:

a)   The space around you shrinks

You would imagine that as time goes on, a corporate would grant you more space; your decision-making power would grow. But the reverse is usually true. Generally, people's remits narrow to their particular domain and they find they are able to do less and less. You're made to feel good by titles of VP or Manager, Expert or Advisor, but those titles also say, 'Here's your sliver of power (don't colour outside the lines)'.

b)   You stop making the decisions

The corporate mechanics of org charts, delegations of authorities and decision rights limit any one person from having too much power. Autonomy is sacrificed because power is shared across dozens or even hundreds of people. Senior people effectively rubber stamp decisions that have been taken lower down in the organization – or at best have to pick one of the three options presented (ideally the one marked 'Recommended Option'). Power is largely limited to sending something back for 'rework'.

c) You slow down

Corporates are compared to tankers because they can find it hard to change course. Decisions can take months and even years. Projects can slip a quarter without raising an eyebrow. The bigger the decision, the more people need to be involved, so decisions can take forever. Very often no decision is reached or it's deferred to await more information or to engage more stakeholders. And, although it can be deeply frustrating, you accept it, you laugh about it, you end up planning for it. You stop fighting for what's needed, you weaken. You accept average.

And what do you think happens, when your space shrinks, your autonomy declines and you begin to accept average and apathy?

Yup – your confidence is gradually eroded.

Stephanie's story

Stephanie got the news late one Friday afternoon – her role had not been designed into the new organization and it was 'in-scope' for redundancy. After 18 years working for the same company, she'd become used to the ebbs and flows of it growing and shrinking. But because she was a specialist individual contributor in a key finance function she'd always been safe.

And because she'd always been safe, she was utterly thrown by the news. She couldn't believe the company could do without her – no-one else had the skills she had, no-one had the experience. She had written the company group practice on her specialist subject for goodness sake. Everyone came to her for advice. Even people outside the firm.

Stephanie had unwittingly grown to believe she was more valuable to the company than she really was. Over almost two decades, she'd committed the cardinal corporate sin of believing she was indispensable.

And she assumed her company felt a high degree of loyalty to her – which she dutifully reciprocated. She'd not once looked for a new job in the 18 years she was there.

For several weeks Stephanie felt betrayed by the company. And by the management of the company. But over time, she began to process how distorted her feelings had become about herself and her employer.

Once she recognized her false frame of reference, she was able to develop a more healthy, positive mindset about her employer and the opportunities she had been given to develop scarce and valuable skills.

Once detached from her corporate job, Stephanie could move on. And she did, to set up her own training consultancy, helping staff in corporates (including the one she had left behind) to learn and practise the specialist skills she had mastered.

All this is nuanced of course. You might actually feel very confident in the job you do each day.

Just don't look too far outside.

You may not realize you've lost your confidence until you face the threat of redundancy – or you think about leaving. And then have to compete in the world outside.

Job cuts, restructuring, new performance criteria, mergers, new bosses, new owners – these pull the rug out from your comfy slippers and make you ask the one question no-one dares to ask about themselves:

Would anyone else want me?

Employment as a transaction

Corporates exist to make money – and, until AI (artificial intelligence) gets a lot better – they need people to make that happen.

They want to get the most value possible from your skills, experience and know-how for the minimum cost.

It's a transaction.

The total cost for them includes Salary + Benefits + Development opportunities.

Salary and Benefits are obvious and easy to measure, but Development opportunities are a grey area. There are times when you may accept a lower salary for development that will become more valuable to you later on and increase your salary.

But, in general, formal development tends to decline for most roles after a few years. It switches to 'on the job' training. Experience starts to count for more than qualifications.

Note, in the employer's costs there's no mention of loyalty of the kind Stephanie gave and expected in return.

Which is a shame, because it actually might be a big part of the value you're adding – building stability, coaching the next generation, going above and beyond.

Loyalty is what often makes the relationship unbalanced.

Because if it's not reciprocated, resentment can creep in. Which can be a terrible thing for confidence.

Balance in the relationship with your employer is key. It should be a loveless marriage of convenience, rational and equitable.

It can't be any other way really because the company isn't a real thing, with feelings. It can't love, or be loyal or even grateful. No matter what the Purpose and Values team try to make you believe.

The proof of this is if you do leave, you'll be replaced. And because of all the great benefits of working for corporates, it won't take long.

I don't want to get all Marxist but you are just a worker. You can be replaced relatively easily by others. The War for Talent isn't universal and with another billion people being added to the planet, there are plenty of people ready to fill your shoes. And that's before you think about the robots.

So that's the reality check. If you're giving up more than you're getting, you need to do something about it.

Start by being honest with yourself. It's part of detaching from your corporate job and your reliance on it as your only option. It certainly isn't.

Corporates aren't evil (usually); they're just an efficient way to organize resources to create value and generate profit. Whilst they don't really care, if you're lucky, there are people working within those companies who do care. But they also have shrinking space, limited control and are frustrated by the glacial pace of decision-making.

They might even be reading this book too, plotting their escape.

So, this is on you.

It always was. But now you need to face it.

And while you're there, start to become a bit more optimistic about the opportunities you have too – and the incredible things you can do because of the skills, experience and know-how you've developed working for corporates.

Exercise 1 is designed to get both sides of your brain focused on what you give up and get from your current job. Remember, all the exercises and templates are free to download from corporateescapology.com/tools.

Exercise 1: The Balanced Corporate Equation

Exercise instructions

Step 1	In the left-hand boxes jot down some things you get out of your job. Start with the obvious ones like salary, benefits, training. Then think a bit more abstractly, e.g. status, identity, stability – be as specific as you can.
Step 2	In the right-hand boxes, add some of the things that you give up because of your job, like time, energy, skills, experience. I think it's good to be tough on yourself on the right-hand side of the equation. And a bit cynical – just to build a really honest picture of what you are giving up to access what you're getting.
	For example, for a long time I gave up some of my entrepreneurial ambition as a trade for predictable income. I also gave up my need for variety and autonomy. And I gave up some of my principles about the kind of people with whom I wanted to work, because I couldn't choose my colleagues or leaders. I gave up on almost all my sense of purpose.

Step 3 Finally, turn it into an equation – circle the >, =, < sign that best fits. And ask yourself why? Is one element playing a disproportionate role?

The Balanced Corporate Equation

What I get from my job

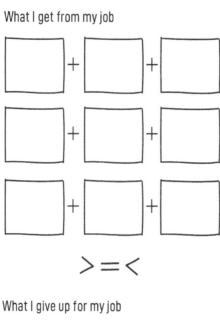

$$> = <$$

What I give up for my job

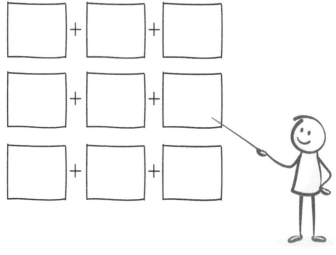

Chapter summary

O   Getting into a corporate is an achievement that should be celebrated.

O   Working in a corporate brings many benefits and opportunities.

O   Skills, experience and potential value creation are exchanged for salary, benefits and development.

O   Autonomy and control are traded in exchange for stability.

O   Working in a corporate environment can negatively impact confidence over time.

O   The relationship between corporate and employee should be a marriage of convenience, not based on human emotions like loyalty, gratitude or love.

O   You are responsible for your own future – and you have the wherewithal to build it as you choose.

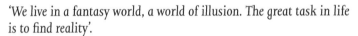

CHAPTER 2

The world today and what's changed

'We live in a fantasy world, a world of illusion. The great task in life is to find reality'.

Iris Murdoch, Author

Context is everything. And if that context is the four walls of a corporate, everything inside those four walls becomes super-important, at least for the hours you're at work (and often for much of the time outside as well).

It's culture – how things work here. You start fitting in as soon as you join – or you don't, and you don't last too long. Most people fit in – they're recruited that way. Early frictions ease and they learn to play the game.

Another way of saying this is we become institutionalized. Over 16 years in my last company, I now see I was pretty institutionalized – the coded language, the acronyms, the ways to get things done, the ways to avoid, the people to avoid. And the overwhelming sense that this was <u>everything</u>. This was important. It was worthwhile. It fuelled me.

And while I was there it was (mostly) true; as soon as I left, I realized it was almost all untrue. And as for the fuel, that was me – and it still is today.

From the outside, everything inside a corporate looks pretty small. Much less important, much less purposeful, and frankly, much less worthwhile. Sorry.

It's easy to over-inflate the importance of your own company in the world, and your role within it.

This chapter is about waking up to the world outside, what has changed and why it's both a bit scary and hugely exciting. It's also where I'll present a case for how the changing world needs things that corporate people, like you, are well placed to deliver.

What's changed?

I started working for corporates early on as a Saturday Lad at British retailer John Lewis, hauling giant TVs into the back of people's cars, then on the shop floor as a student and then after university I joined its graduate training scheme. I absolutely loved it. I embraced the regimented breaks, the training, the language, the uniform, the hierarchy and how different level managers sat in different zones of the dining room. I loved knowing the rules, fitting in, being an insider.

Part way through the graduate training scheme I woke up from the stupor and broke free. I have never forgotten my line manager (herself a graduate high-flyer) literally bashing her head on the table as I broke the news to her. I went back to university to do a Masters and from there moved into consulting for lots of corporates – Reuters, BT, BA, BP and an 18-month secondment to the UK Cabinet Office.

I left consulting and joined BP in 2006, so for more than 25 years I'd only ever known big company cultures, and to be honest they all looked pretty similar. BP even had subsidized lunches, its own stately homes you could visit for away-days, and even more rules than John Lewis. In days gone by at BP, you had different carpet around your desk if you were a manager or executive. Now it's just the share options.

Outside these safe and stately corporates, however, the world looks very different. Some really seismic shifts have been underway over the past two decades.

Macro changes affecting the world of work

1   Globalization has opened our minds to diverse cultures, better business practices and created opportunities. It has also exposed and widened differences, encouraging the worst excesses of capitalism and greed, with most of the eight billion people on the planet systemically disadvantaged.

2   Technology has disrupted whole industries, changing the nature of jobs for millions. Some people can work from anywhere, most people cannot.

3   An 'always-on' culture, fuelled by social media, 24-hour TV and email, has brought information to our fingertips, delivered instant gratification and contributed to a growing mental health crisis.

4   Flexible contracting with workers has created opportunities for some but it has destabilized many more.

5   Legislative, regulatory and social pressures to act on everything, from climate change to issues of diversity, equity and inclusion, are impacting many businesses, some even existentially.

On top of these macro changes there are other trends that feel more personal but which, at scale, have profoundly, maybe permanently, affected how we view work and our employers.

Trends in how we feel about work

(In)gratitude

As a child of the 1980s, I grew up with the view that we should be thankful for our benevolent employer for giving us a job. The uncertainties at the time caused by strikes and deregulation didn't directly hit me or my family, as they did entire communities (and still do today), but they contributed to a sense of 'get a job, lay low, don't cause trouble – and for goodness sake show some gratitude'.

That's changed. Generally speaking, Millennial and Gen Z people recognize, quite rightly, that the employment contract is mutual; loyalty is fairly weak and lock-in serves few of us well. Even my 'Must try harder' Generation X feels less of the instinctive gratitude to an employer than it once did.

But sometimes the ingratitude can cause us to expect too much, making unrealistic demands of an organization also trying to satisfy thousands of other stakeholders with similarly unrealistic expectations.

Purpose

This is a relatively recent trend perhaps born out of a moderating reaction to the worst excesses of capitalism. 'Shareholder value' doesn't get many of us out of bed each day. A new breed of more purposeful organizations grew up in the 2000s and in the years which followed. Indeed, many of today's tech Goliaths started life positioning themselves as purposeful disrupters of the Goliaths of the day.

Today, most big companies have jumped on the purpose bandwagon. Everyone's got one now: 'Build a better tomorrow™' is British American Tobacco's.

Connecting workforces to something deeper and more meaningful is pretty obvious. It's worked for millions of small and medium-sized businesses for decades, but it's relatively new for corporates.

I desperately tried to connect with my company's purpose, I really did. But it was pretty hopeless. Corporate purpose may be well-intentioned, but it is almost always too generic and high-level to have meaning for most of us as individuals.

Authenticity

Social trends often emerge because their opposite becomes so unappealing that sections of society rise up and demand change. Authenticity has become important because of a perceived lack of it – in our politicians, in the marketing we unconsciously consume, in our relationships on and offline. And in the employing organizations to which we commit, where we spend a third of our lives – and often much more.

The phrase Authentic Leadership has become hackneyed, and yet it remains far from the norm. Possibly it's the reality of what it really takes to get on in big business and the sacrifices decent people feel they need to make to progress.

In most cases we're not seeing it.

Flexibility

The '9 to 5' may well be dead, but only because we now work much earlier and later, with work often intruding into the weekends and holidays. We don't really want to, but we just do – because others do, because it's easier to answer the email in the bathroom after the starter, so we can enjoy our main course with friends.

You can email me on a Sunday night and I can choose whether to respond. I probably will feel obliged if it's from my boss or my boss's boss. But I may knock off early on a Friday. Or I might work late in the evening, if I'm able to drop the kids into school the next day. Or I might even change my work patterns or reduce my hours. There's more flexibility than ever before.

But there's an urge among many employers to limit it.

These huge macro forces, multiplied by the trends in how we feel about work, have been accelerating since the 1960s, and most strikingly since the 1980s. But nothing has affected society so dramatically as the COVID-19 pandemic of 2020–2022 when how we lived, not just worked, changed fundamentally, and, in some cases, perhaps irrevocably.

Life in a pandemic

It's a heading I would never have expected to use. Pandemics happen somewhere else. And yet this one happened everywhere. The clue is in the prefix I suppose. When we were in it every part of our life seemed to change. Not being able to leave the house, the fear of meeting people you knew or didn't know, home-schooling, not knowing when it would end – all of these things transformed society at the time and they still ripple on. When we were inside it, it felt very much like history in the making, something children would learn about in school. If they ever went back to school, which some did not.

And, of course, work changed profoundly:

○ We proved we could work flexibly

The technology held up – even if we had to turn our cameras off when five of us all needed to be on Teams or Google Classroom (or Netflix) at the same time. Many companies, like my own, had been preparing for this kind of risk (they probably assumed it would be terrorism or war rather than a global pandemic). But there was, for many of us, an unexpected degree of resilience.

And so, the same recurring weekly meetings carried on, where we swapped notes on how we were coping. More emails and WhatsApps were sent and received, and slightly awkward attempts at online social events were made. We kept calm (ok, not always) and carried on. Many people were juggling home-schooling or caring for others and working from home, so technology enabled a degree of flexibility in when and how we got our jobs done.

○ We saw our employers at their best (and worst)

The pandemic was a very human experience. Indeed, some people look back quite fondly to an uptick in care, empathy and sympathy for our fellow human beings. The phrase #selfcare trended everywhere – and we gained insight into the lives of our colleagues, friends and families that we may not have had before.

With authority figures at that time on a war-footing (who could forget those daily podium briefings?), employers followed suit, with more assertive language, new policies and rules how to cope. But also, there was a shift for some in how they treated their staff.

Flexibility over work patterns, with greater understanding if some people dropped out of calls, or entire days, if they were coping with challenges at home. There was a much greater focus and appreciation of the impact of the pandemic on mental health, with support on hand, training and services (for some).

Many people have only great things to say about how their organizations and their leaders behaved during the pandemic, how the company values were tested and how the company rose to exceed all expectations.

But not everybody. Some people saw a less appealing side of their employer – or their line manager – which surfaced under the pressure of the lockdowns. A company's response to a crisis is always in two parts: 1) the official rules, policies and decisions and 2) the individual behaviours and actions by leaders and peers. Some companies showed their true colours by sacking whole sections of the workforce, properly dispelling any myth of the benevolent employer, 'there for you' in a crisis. Stories of bullying, exclusion, discrimination, intolerance, unkindness, retaliation, etc. were widespread, published on digital platforms where unhappy staff could vent. Some companies came out of the experience very poorly.

o   We saw how short life is and asked, 'what if'?

Confronted by horrifying charts, each day, enumerating recorded deaths, our outlook contracted to the very near-term. The climate crisis dropped into second place as the biggest perceived threat to human life. And so, once we had developed partial coping strategies to deal with the daily media frenzy, once we had got through the home-schooling and caring alongside juggling our jobs, many people began to question whether it was all really worth it?

For some people, the answer was no – they sold up and moved to the beach or the country. Many started side-hustles (finding time from goodness knows where), others gave up their jobs entirely. Very few decided they'd missed their calling to be teachers.

Confronted by the pandemic, we wailed 'There must be more to life than this'.

The combination of these factors, during and just after the pandemic, prompted many people to leave their jobs. The 'Great Resignation' was real: in the United States 20% more people left their jobs in 2021 and 2022 than in 2018 and 2019[2] (it was about the same increase in the UK[3]). In the US they cited reasons like feeling disrespected at work, a lack of flexibility and limited career advancement options[4]. In short, they'd had enough of their employers, they wanted more flexibility and they wanted greater fulfilment.

Today, many people are working more flexibly than ever before – trying to find more balance or 'blend' in their life between home and work, and the pandemic has increased their need for purpose. I think of it very much as a one-way trend that's been going on for decades, easily since the 1980s, if not the 1960s… but the pandemic accelerated changes and for many, those changes will never be reversed.

I want to add a note about privilege at this point. I do recognize that much of the experience I have described here will only resonate with a privileged section of society in reasonably well-paid, stable jobs. Those who before the pandemic faced unrelenting job insecurity, enforced zero-hours contracts, multiple jobs to make ends meet, financial pressures, unstable housing and uncomfortable lives were doubtless a lot worse off through the pandemic. They were unlikely to find benevolent employers granting flexibility, choice, support and all the other luxuries many of us experienced in our corporate jobs.

In many ways the life I lead in my late 40s is quite different from the one I led in my 20s, with a brick for a phone, a Hotmail address and a Netscape CD. But there's always continuity as well as change – and although we might look at the world today as one radically different from the one our parents and grandparents lived in at our age, the changes have been coming for decades. They have just been accelerated by globalization, by technology and more rapidly by the pandemic.

---

[2] U.S. Bureau of Labor Statistics' Job Openings and Labor Turnover Survey, 2022.

[3] Office for National Statistics (UK); Q1 2001 to Q2 2023; 16-69 years.

[4] Great Resignation, Pew Research Center, 2022.

You may not like all of these changes. Undoubtedly some are not for the better. But this is the world in which you live.

And remember, it's your choice how you engage with it.

This is a good opportunity to pause and reflect on how you may have changed since you started your corporate career – or even how you have changed over the past few years (see Exercise 2).

Not all these factors affect everyone equally. Which do you feel most strongly about? Which are prompting you to seek change?

Exercise 2: How I've Changed

Exercise instructions

Step 1	In the left-hand box, jot down some work-related factors that are more important to you today than they once were – they may be flexibility or stability, or something specific like childcare. Perhaps it's something deeper like purpose or feeling valued as an expert.
Step 2	In the right-hand box write down what is less important than it once was. Maybe it's career advancement or bonuses. Maybe it's being a people manager.
Step 3	What do you notice or observe about these changes? How are they affecting how you feel about yourself and your work?

How we view our corporate jobs today

The sad fact is that many people aren't as happy in their corporate careers as they once were. They aren't as engaged, despite more investment than ever in employee communications, values programmes and all manner of incentives.

According to Gallup's *State of the Global Workplace*, only 23% of employees are engaged at work. This global average masks some country-specific employee engagement problems: in the UK it's 10%, in France it's 7% and in Italy and Japan it's just 5%. The US, interestingly, registers a lot higher engagement at 32%.

How I've Changed

Things that are **more** important to me now

Things that are **less** important to me now

Observations

The same report suggests that 51% of currently employed workers around the world say they are 'actively seeking a new job or watching for openings'.

That is staggering! Half of the people you work with would like to be in a different job this time next year.

Job motivation appears to be slipping, shown by the CIPD's *Good Work Index 2023* which recorded a 7% increase in agreement to the statement that 'a job was just a means of making money'; it has increased from 36% in 2019 to 43% in 2023. The share who said they were willing to work harder to help their employer fell from 57% to 51%.

Trends like 'Quiet Quitting' (where employees appear to avoid work) and 'Lazy Girl' (where female employees prioritize life over work) transcend geographical boundaries and demonstrate incontrovertibly that our relationship with work has changed.

In this context, how you feel about your job may be quite normal, part of a much bigger global trend to feel less happy at work, less fulfilled and less likely to believe it's the only career pathway.

But don't get down-hearted.

What you can do that others can't

For all this gloom, let's get one thing straight: the world needs corporate people – preferably engaged, ideally not spending all their time looking for a new job.

Time working in corporate environments confers unique advantages on you that others simply don't have. **This is a central tenet of this book: you are valuable and people outside your corporate job think so too.** Even if, like you, they may have fewer positive views of the corporates for whom you have worked.

Corporate people see, approach and act on things in a different way from people who have worked in SMEs (Small and Medium Sized Enterprises), Startups, Not-for-profits and even Government – and that can create value for others.

You have been trained to think in a particular way, mainly through your work culture. You quickly learnt how one set of behaviours and actions was rewarded and another set was punished.

You learn these things quite unconsciously – and assume everyone else knows them too. But they don't. They are learnt behaviours. Often over many years.

Not reading the room keeps you out of the room. Poor attention to detail gets you side-lined. A glaring omission in your strategy presentation humiliates your manager (with consequences later on for you). And claiming success on inputs rather than outcomes is frankly naive.

You learn these things fast in a corporate. In the school of hard knocks.

I always remember my top boss coming to me after a pretty big workshop I'd run with a bunch of his peers. 'How do you think that went?', he said. I was pretty green at the time and I focused on all the positives. Which made it all the more awkward for him to tell me all the things he didn't think went well.

Another boss said early on 'You're so fast!' several times before I realized she was actually saying 'You're too fast and your quality is off.'

Learning these subtle cues is how to survive and thrive in a corporate.

And they can be immensely valuable throughout your whole career.

Jack of all Trades, Master of None…

But do you know the rest of the phrase? It's 'Jack of all trades is a master of none, but oftentimes better than a master of one.'

Interestingly, we drop the last bit because it doesn't suit the 'cult of the expert'.

For a long time, maybe still today, 'generalist' was a bad word in a corporate. It made you vulnerable. There was a huge pull to functionalize with everything linked to narrowly defined specialisms.

I hated it. I am a classic generalist, even though I spent most of my career in marketing. My last company didn't have a marketing function, so I was an orphan, surrounded by super-technical specialists, many of whom were world leaders in their fields. At times it was uncomfortable, but mostly I liked being different and complementary to others.

But even those super-technical folks could make a PowerPoint, build a spreadsheet, write a strategy, run a workshop, etc. They, like me, were 'T-shaped', with a broad top and a long column. Today, it's all the rage – T-shaped people know a few things very, very well and lots of things well enough.

This is likely to be you. Or most of you. Even if you are a distinguished advisor or a technical specialist, you won't have got far without generalist skills to sell, negotiate, explain, enrol, reposition and a dozen other things besides.

The seminal work on Generalists is David Epstein's *Range* (*Why Generalists Triumph in a Specialized World*), which I really recommend. He compares Tiger Woods' hyperspecialization with Roger Federer's generalist approach (trying lots of sports before settling on tennis) – and he's a fan of the latter.

The world's biggest challenges (think climate change, geopolitics, social inequality, AI) require strategic thinkers, with the capacity to take on and integrate diverse, and potentially conflicting, data to solve problems – David Epstein writes, 'The bigger the picture, the more unique the potential human contribution. Our greatest strength is the exact opposite of narrow specialization. It is the ability to integrate broadly.'

It's this blend of generalist with specialist that makes corporate people very marketable. You've got the experience, the safe pairs of hands, the context, the understanding of people and politics and lots of other skills, experience and know-how that make you trusted, quick to get going and highly valuable for a broad range of modern-day opportunities.

You're going to work on identifying your own unique blend of skills, experience and know-how, as well as what you might do with them next, over the coming chapters, but first you need to address any bad thinking you may be carrying – it's time to ditch the corporate baggage.

Chapter summary

o The world of work today feels quite different from the world of our parents – with dramatic shifts in technology, globalization and attitudes.

o The COVID-19 pandemic accelerated many changes, rendering some irreversible.

o Some of these challenges exposed or increased weaknesses in the relationship between employer and employee.

○ Corporates tend to be viewed quite negatively from the outside, and increasingly from the inside, with employee engagement at new lows.

○ There are clusters of capabilities that are unique to people who have worked in corporate roles and they can create exceptional and unique value for others.

CHAPTER 3

Dismantling myths

'The lies we tell other people are nothing to the lies we tell ourselves.'

Derek Landy, Author

In my research for this book, I began to notice something rather concerning.

People in corporate jobs – regardless of sector, seniority or specialism – carry some dangerous myths.

I did too.

They need to be dispelled before you can move on.

Myth 1: You are your job title and your role

Many people accept what they do at work as all they can do. Because they introduce themselves by their job title, it begins to define them – and limit them.

For a long time, I described myself as 'Marketing Director' because I felt that job title was the best fit for the work I did. But in one restructure, the term 'Director' was banned, so 'Directors' became 'Managers'. In a later restructure, 'Manager' was only reserved for those managing teams. In both cases I ignored the rules because I wanted that job title as it held meaning for others, internally and externally – and, I'll admit, it was validating for me.

However, that Marketing Director role typically took up about 60% of my time. For the remainder, I was at various times running culture change programmes, acting as an executive's assistant, managing internal communications, leading a strategy project, coaching a bunch of people – the list goes on. And I didn't really give myself credit for this.

'Marketing Director' was a simple moniker, but it was not an accurate description of all I did or could do. That was never written down.

Having talked to people who have left corporate jobs, my experience is far from unique. It may be one you also recognize.

More dangerous and insidious than thinking your job title is what you do, is *feeling* like it's all you <u>can</u> do, and worse, like you can't do anything else – you're not capable, need permission or authority, lack the experience or potential.

It's nonsense, but it's quite normal if you've been wearing that job title for a while.

Listen to me: You are far more than your job title or job description. You are everything you can do, what you know and what you've got the capacity to do. You are in control of defining who you are and who you want to be.

Myth 1 debunked.

Myth 2: You've got too much to lose to leave

It's brave to do something new, especially something big, like leave your job. It's normal to feel scared and overwhelmed by the risk.

But many corporate people have been conditioned to see risk as something that needs to be eliminated or avoided altogether. When in fact it is a normal part of life, closely linked to our growth and development.

However, for the avoidance of doubt, the risk of leaving your job is real, it's not a myth.

The myth is that leaving is reckless and only has downside risk.

If you walk out without any preparation, both might be true.

But you're not going to do that. You're going to dispassionately evaluate each risk for impact and probability, using your corporate training, and clarify the necessary practical steps to manage those risks until they're acceptable for the return. And you're going to do this before you leave.

Some corporate people fear giving up just before the pay-off; the Big Leader role that has been dangled before their eyes ever since they joined: 'Another year and I'll get my dues'.

For most people, let's be honest, that never happens. Even if they spend all career trying. That's one corporate myth I'm not going to attempt to dispel.

Anticipated regret is when we project forward and imagine how we will feel about something that happens (or doesn't happen). Used wisely it can be a superpower to prevent bad things happening – but it can also keep us stuck.

If you want to learn more about regret read Dan Pink's *The Power of Regret*, based on his survey of over 19,000 people across the world. His analysis shows that more people regret not having done something than having done something – twice as many in fact. In other words, inaction is a bigger driver of regret than action.

And, by the way, regrets around careers were the fourth most common, after regrets about family, partners and education.

You have been warned.

Myth 3: No-one wants you

Imposter syndrome is boringly predictable. It kicks in whenever we do something new – before we have to prove ourselves. It's linked to flight, when our survival is under threat, and it's really there to protect us. We need to thank it but send it on its way.

In Chapter 2 I talked about the gradual erosion of self-confidence when we stay in the same job too long, with shrinking space, reduced power and the insidious acceptance of slow and average.

This can lead you to wonder if you have value outside. I have seen people literally hide during restructures through fear they'll be 'found out' if they're forced outside the company.

And yet, time and time again I see the opposite: corporate experience is valued, it brings credibility and corporate people can do things others cannot.

In the immortal words of Kojak, you have to know 'Who loves ya, baby?'. My experience is that corporate people don't always fit well with early-stage startups; there tends to be a culture clash of expectations and standards. But as a startup scales up, corporate people can be valuable and build confidence in investors; they can add tremendous value for small and medium sized businesses too. As you will see in Part III, corporate people make excellent consultants, fulfilling a broad spectrum of needs, as well as coaches, freelancers, authors, experts, board advisors, mentors, etc.

They – you – can do many things better, faster, safer… the list goes on.

We'll work more on busting Myth 3 in Chapter 5, but for now put it on the Parking Lot.

Myth 4: You're only cut out for corporates

Inside a corporate, everyone practises becoming really successful at a small number of things. Everything else is left to others: Finance picks up the invoicing, Procurement the contracts, HR the people stuff, Marketing the messaging, etc.

It's a particular way of working that operates in only very large organizations working at scale. Not only would it be really hard for someone in Marketing to do anything in Finance, but the turf wars would kick off if you tried.

So, Marketers stay in Marketing, Lawyers in Legal, Accountants in Finance. Everyone learns to become successful managing their own cog of the operation.

Faced with the prospect of leaving their cog to join a startup, or become a consultant, or set up a social enterprise, or build a business, it's no surprise that many fall victim to Myth 4 ('I'm only cut out to be a corporate') and retreat to safety.

I'm here to tell you it's narrow thinking. It assumes you can't learn something you don't know or find a way to outsource it. In my experience working with corporate people, even if they haven't run businesses, they have extremely good business nous. And they're tenacious, resourceful and usually much more versatile than they give themselves credit.

Mastering something new might take time of course. But no-one is entirely cut out for one thing, everyone can adapt.

And it's definitely not a reason to stay put.

So, that's four classic myths I've heard time and time again – explicitly and implicitly – since I've been working with corporate people thinking about leaving.

During my years in corporates and consultancies, I always spent time mentoring, talking to people about their dreams and plans, helping open their minds, trying to make them see what I saw.

Now I look back, most of my conversations with bright, capable and successful people were rooted in these myths, these fears, which kept many of them from realizing their potential and following their dreams.

They are self-limiting narratives. And it's time to offload them now (see Exercise 3).

Exercise 3: Offloading The Baggage

Exercise instructions

Step 1	We all have gremlins, imposter syndrome, internal critics, self-limiting beliefs. Just imagine you're handing in your notice tomorrow morning, think of all the reasons you'll fail.
	This is your Bad Thinking – write it down in the left-hand box.
Step 2	Now you need to step into the shoes of your kinder self, or even a good friend, and flip that Bad Thinking.
	For each line of Bad Thinking, write its opposite in the right-hand box under Good Thinking.
	For example, some of my Bad Thinking was 'I was lucky to get this job – I'll be found out somewhere else'. Flipped to Good Thinking, this becomes 'I got hired on my potential, but now have a proven track record to offer others'.
	And more Bad Thinking 'I'm too corporate to be an entrepreneur' flipped to much better Good Thinking 'I'm going to become my own type of entrepreneur leveraging my corporate background'.
Step 3	Cover the Bad Thinking side of the table with your hand and just read the Good Thinking. Ask yourself what would it take for you to believe this? Do your friends and colleagues believe this about you already? How would it feel if <u>you</u> believed it?

You may not fully believe this Good Thinking yet but keep revisiting this page. Fold over the corner. There's a little 'fake it 'til you become it' needed here just to get you to break the cycle of Bad Thinking.

Offloading The Baggage

Bad thinking		Good thinking
	>	
	>	
	>	
	>	
	>	

This exercise reminds me a little of one of my favourite TED Talks, with Amy Cuddy – *Your body language may shape who you are*. Amy presents research that supports how posing more assertively and confidently, even for a few minutes, ahead of a stressful situation like a presentation or interview can make us feel more confident, as shown in our brain's chemistry.

You can argue the science, as many have done since the original TED Talk, but the combination of positive self-talk, visualization and posture feels like a solid formula for holding back the gremlins long enough for you to start believing in yourself.

Now you've got your Good Thinking written down, you can use it to start believing in yourself.

Chapter summary

○ Time in a corporate career may lead to Bad Thinking myths that can perpetuate and become deeply entrenched.

○ These myths tend to lead to limiting beliefs which stop successful people believing they can work anywhere other than the corporate environment.

○ These myths need to be dispelled in order to make progress.

○ Consciously flipping unhelpful or limiting beliefs into more positive, progressive thinking can help generate the traction required to detach and define an alternative future.

CHAPTER 4

On the veranda

'Nostalgia is a seductive liar.'

George Ball, Politician

My coach gave me this phrase 'on the veranda' when I'd left my comfy corporate job and started looking back, a bit longingly.

Picture the scene after your leaving party, where everyone has been patting you on the back, telling you how brave you are for leaving (you'll get a lot of that), toasting your success. But the sun has gone down now and it's got a bit chilly. You find yourself outside but now you're on your own. Looking out into the dark, open nothingness.

Gulp.

And what's worse, you look back into the party room (that's your old job) and everyone is having fun, everything is familiar, it's warm and bright. Everyone is so damn happy. And quite smug.

And you think 'I want that'. You might even find yourself hammering on the door.

But no-one will let you in. They can't even hear you now.

Don't worry, the veranda moment doesn't last long. Because the image isn't real. It's a rose-tinted, nostalgic view of all the very best bits of your old job, without a single bad bit (and there were some, weren't there?).

However, do learn from my mistake of not being prepared for this veranda moment. Multiple moments. Sometimes it hits me still today, although less and less. Because the idea of safety, even if it's boring, debilitating and not what we really want, feels good when we're feeling uncomfortable.

The trick is to be ready for the veranda moment, so you recognize it and know how to deal with it. Like having a Patronus handy to face-off a Dementor.

This chapter deals with the things that might join you on the veranda when you're feeling a little low: what you're leaving behind, the identity crisis, the sense of rejection. But don't worry, we're going to end more positively with an exercise to understand the forces that are pushing you off that veranda and upwards, into the bright, optimistic life that awaits you.

What you're leaving behind

In the 20 odd years working for corporates, I have never met a single person who left their job and regretted leaving, eventually. Of course, you can always catch people at a bad time. But it's human nature to keep moving forward – and to focus on positives.

So, even if there are difficult times, you'll eventually build a narrative that validates your decision and look back knowing you're in a better place than before.

There are, however, some real things you are leaving behind. And you need to come to terms with them before you move, because they may be more important to you than you realize – and you will need to work around them or replace them.

The first big thing you're leaving behind is structure and routine
It's one of the most banal aspects of corporate life – the Monday mornings, the Tuesday weekly team meetings, the traipse for lunch, the afternoon meetings that you can only book from 2pm. And before 4pm, because by then the early birds are heading home.

Some things you could literally time your watch by: my favourite was two minutes before 10am each Tuesday there would be a rush for a pitstop and a cup of tea.

For many years I worked in an open-plan office where you could see dozens of people act out the ritual, like automatons.

And the same thing a few hours later, heading for the lunch queue.

Not unlike my kids at school. Just saying.

Millions of people all over the world acting exactly the same way at the same times.

But now as I write this, I feel a tiny bit of nostalgia for those days, those routines. It was simpler, easier, I always knew what I was doing. I felt safe, in my comfy slippers.

When you leave it's not like that.

The only routines and structures you'll have are the ones you create for yourself. You set your own culture. You have to buy your own slippers.

At first that can be hard. And if you lack self-discipline, it can be really hard. Because as anyone who's been on holiday for more than a week knows, it's actually pretty easy to fill your day doing precisely nothing. And not even realize it.

My wife was worried I'd go into my study and bury myself in 'paperwork' and never talk to anyone. She knows that under pressure I can dial up my introverted side and avoid human contact. But just as I left my job, the pandemic hit and the working world was shifting to Microsoft Teams, so everyone went digital.

It was a good thing for me, because as I was finding my feet and exploring how to use my time, the frictions associated with booking face-to-face meetings and going for coffee in London were suddenly removed. Plus, most people were pretty bored, so would happily spend half an hour on the phone.

And for the most part, that's stayed true today: almost all of my meetings are on Zoom. People are generally curious enough to spend half an hour with a stranger they can look up first on LinkedIn.

In the early days, having a few calls lined up helped me to structure my week so I didn't waste time (and then berate myself for it). On quiet weeks, it still has the same effect.

There's no denying that leaving corporate life removes some of that daily, monthly, quarterly, and even annual, business rhythm, which creates momentum, as well as structure. For some people, it's hard to get going, but of course it's possible to learn. And survival eventually kicks in, because clients and partners in your new life expect you to be dressed by 9am.

I've added some ideas for how to build structure into your life in Chapter 13. But for now, project forward to when you've left. Is the lack of structure and routine likely to be a problem? Do you need to do anything now to ease the transition and remove the temptation of staying in bed until midday? Will you need to impose structure to be effective? Could your need for routine, structure and accountability influence what you do next?

The second big thing you're leaving behind is salary
Not just the cash value, but also the predictability, the fact it comes in every month on the same day, regular as clockwork. And moreover, it's what your salary unlocks: your lifestyle and, to a degree, your status.

Access to credit is much easier for a mortgage or a car loan if you can show a track record of receiving a stable salary.

You will probably need to work out how you're going to afford to leave. Part of your preparation may be building a back-up fund, or securing some contract work, or something part-time. You might find a way to make money from a side-hustle without even leaving – the ultimate Minimum Viable Product. Or you might get lucky with a pay-off.

A friend of mine, Sarra (who did the very first review of this book – thank you Sarra!), told me that although she freelanced for more than ten years, she never felt as comfortable as a contractor as when she was salaried because the tax bit was so opaque and it left her anxious. Money is deeply personal – and you need to find out what works for you and avoid what doesn't.

We're going to cover this in a lot more detail in Chapter 6, because the risk of losing a predictable income can be enough to keep most people in their corporate jobs, even if they're unhappy.

But it needn't be, as you'll see.

The third thing you're leaving behind is people
It's a cliché to say you miss the people when you move on. Can it really be true? If you really missed them you could easily find them again. I like meeting up with people I used to work with online or in person, but (sorry) they weren't a reason to keep me doing something I had stopped enjoying. And I hope I wasn't ever a reason for them.

One interesting observation is that formerly corporate people quickly realize that the people left behind were actually rather good.

See! I told you this in the Myths we busted in Chapter 3.

This is also a way of saying people outside are often a lot worse – which is quite harsh. But going back to what I said in the Myths, corporate people are usually really smart and capable, and in most cases they care about quality. You quickly see this when someone does some work for you, like a freelancer or, dare I say it, a client, and you realize how much you have to do to make things look good.

So, I'd say yes, you will have to leave some people behind, but you will see the ones you like again. You only fall off the planet metaphorically when you leave your corporate job, you're still around for meetups.

So that's three things you'll leave behind, but there are two bigger challenges to deal with that may hit you full-force when you're on that veranda: identity crisis and rejection.

Let's look each of them straight in the eye now and face them down.

Identity crisis

Part of the veranda moment is driven by a change in identity, possibly even an identity crisis. When I left university, I worked for a mid-size management consultancy. Because it wasn't one of the big consulting firms, few people had heard of it. I got sick of explaining who they were and what they did (and why I hadn't joined one of the big ones). After five years I left and joined a small boutique strategy consultancy and it was worse. I felt like I had to justify myself, as well as my employer.

When I joined BP, it was different. For 16 years, when someone asked me 'What do you do?' it was enough to say, 'I work for BP'. Rarely was there a follow-up question.

I can only assume it was for one of three reasons:

1   Maybe they thought I worked in a petrol forecourt and didn't know what the next question should be (unlikely).

2   Maybe they hated oil companies (quite likely).

3   Maybe the answer said enough for them about the kind of person I was (most likely).

BP quickly became a major part of my identity.

When I left 16 years later, it was like a part of me had been removed. I went to a startup pitch event recently, with investors and other corporates. I had my badge on for the accelerator programme I run, but it wasn't a well-known name. And I had to puff out my chest a bit more.

When I was at BP, I was lazy. People wanted to talk to me.

Just having the name on my badge created an opportunity for someone - I could sit back.

Now I can't.

It's tempting to swap one corporate badge for another and then you never face this awkwardness, this vulnerability. But do you really want your identity to be so tied up with something or someone else? Wouldn't you rather have it defined by something you've built, rather than something someone else has built? Something over which you have more control?

Part of the problem is that you can't just swap out your old identity for something new. It can take a while to work out what you're doing and even longer to get comfortable so you can talk about it with confidence.

It will never be as simple to explain what you do as when you could say 'I work for <Insert Household Name>'.

Ambiguity like this can create anxiety, I know.

Associating with what someone else has built provides a security blanket. And without it we're more exposed, less secure. Years later I'm still aware of the gap it's left and how much harder I need to work to define myself and create the space I deserve.

From my coaching, I notice that the clients who have left through redundancy struggle most with their lost identity. It's understandable because their corporate identity has been forcibly removed – in some cases without much notice.

But this is another myth, a fear I'm happy to dispel.

The reality is that none of us lose our identity overnight. It doesn't end as you walk out the door. Much of your credibility, and therefore your identity, travels with you. Years later barely a week passes when I don't mention BP and something I saw, did or learnt there. The startup accelerator programme I run is for Shell, so my BP experience gives me credibility with Shell people as well as with the startups I'm helping.

You can't deny the past and you won't want to because it has helped form the person you are today – as well as what you're able to do next.

In fact, I believe you can hold on to that identity as long as you choose. You'll only drop it if you work for someone better or if you move out of your former employer's industry and your background stops being so relevant.

The point is **you** will decide when your corporate identity ceases to be valuable or useful; until then it's yours to keep using.

In Part IV, we'll work on defining your new identity as you break free, so start thinking now about how you might like to describe what you do.

Rejection

The second big challenge that will probably hit you on the veranda is rejection.

I volunteered for redundancy, but still felt rejected. I half expected (and half wanted) someone to block my Expression of Interest: 'Adam, we can't run BP without you'.

In the month when my application for redundancy was considered, I was on tenterhooks that it would be declined and the new pathways that I was starting to open up would be closed off.

Yet when my boss told me my request had been accepted there was a part of me that thought 'Really? Don't you need me?'.

And that feeling persisted through the first year. Every time I met someone from BP, or I received an email from a former colleague, I felt sure they would say 'Come back, it was all a terrible mistake'. Some people I know did go back as consultants and contractors and I wondered why they weren't asking me.

If they had come to me in that first year, I honestly don't know what I would have said. At vulnerable moments I might have said yes.

And then I would have missed out on the life I'm leading now which I know is better.

I say all this because this is from someone who *volunteered* for redundancy, so for people who haven't volunteered, rejection is frankly unavoidable.

As I said earlier, when you've given so much of your time, some of your passion and maybe even your heart, to a job, you're going to feel rejected when you're told you're no longer required. For some people it's painful and may take months or even years from which to recover.

Rejection at some level connects with shame. It drives straight to the heart of our self-worth. And the worst part is that it's so very public.

Over 30 years later my dad can't say anything positive about the US pharmaceutical giant that acquired his UK pharmaceutical giant. It disbanded the research programme and the plant that he and his team had been building for years. Those feelings run deep.

A proud man, I suspect he felt like he'd let his family down – as well as his team.

I'll never forget one day while I was at university my mum told me he'd gone to the local supermarket to get a job. This was a guy with a PhD and 30 years of experience designing drugs to fight cancer. And he was rejected – again.

The story ends happily as he turned his passion for sailing into a business, making him my original inspiration for life after corporate.

There are better books than this one to help you deal with rejection. There are still better coaches and therapists who can help you work through the hurt and move on.

What this book says though is use those feelings.

Understanding why you care so much will help inform the next chapter of your life. Do you want to ever feel like this again? Are your skills, experience and know-how valued more by others than your former employer? What are you glad to leave behind? What have you learnt about yourself?

I'm a big believer in both coaching and therapy, because I believe they can help you accelerate through intense pain that otherwise will drag you down and slow your progress.

My one piece of advice is don't let rejection feed into your public persona. Never let anyone, apart from your nearest and dearest, think you're carrying rejection baggage. Fake it if you must, but rejection is a millstone; it's toxic and will switch off people who will otherwise do their best to help you.

Remain positive in public. Even if inside you're feeling quite the opposite. This is about helping people to help you, which is the subject of Chapter 10.

Use the force(s)

I feel like we've wallowed enough in the good and the bad things about corporates, as well as what you're leaving behind. You now need to start moving forward and off the veranda.

Part I has been about detaching yourself from corporate life, bringing some objectivity and reason to what you're leaving behind and what you think you might want from what's next.

I've talked about some of the things that may be making you stick with your job, even if you know you can do better. And I've touched on some of the fears and anxieties that keep you rooted to your current situation.

Let's start to summarize how you're feeling, to see whether you are ready to move. Or whether you need more time to prepare.

One of the tools I have developed is called the Forces of Change Model. It builds on pioneering research by Kurt Lewin in the 1950s on *driving forces* and *restraining forces* relating to change.

The model is made up of four parts:

> *Pain: the driving forces that make you want to escape your Current World.*

> *Progress: the driving forces that move you towards a New World (a new job, working for yourself, writing a book, etc.).*

> *Fear: the restraining forces that worry you about that New World.*

> *Safety: the restraining forces that keep you stuck in your Old World.*

The model is underpinned by a simple equation which states that people will only move to a New World if the combined strength of the driving forces (Pain + Progress) is greater than the combined strength of the restraining forces (Fear + Safety), i.e.

If Pain + Progress > Safety + Fear => New World.

If not, you'll stay stuck in your Current World.

Let's dive into each in a bit more detail.

Pain forces make you feel like 'enough is enough': the bureaucracy, the politics, the endless cycles, the lack of autonomy, the feeling you no longer fit, the lack of reward, the misalignment with purpose, the plateauing.

Progress forces connect you with what's possible, who you could be and how it might make you feel. Progress is measured functionally, emotionally and socially – with emotional progress and social progress being most important. Emotional progress is how you want to feel in yourself – free, responsible, purposeful? Social progress is how you want to feel in front of, or with, others – like you belong, positioned as an expert, or treated respectfully?

Safety forces keep you locked to the present, whether that's the certainty of salary, healthcare, bonuses, etc., or the routines you know and value.

Don't be too hard on yourself here – staying put at certain times in your life makes sense. Sometimes it's not worth disrupting what works; it depends on what you value. But Safety forces don't make us happy and they don't tend to quieten our internal voices that demand change.

Fear forces can be perceived or real when considering what the New World might offer – as well as whether it's possible. It's best to get all these fears out on the table, as you don't want them creeping up on you at 3am when you're tired and vulnerable. Fears around income, your skills, network, confidence, self-discipline and ten thousand other things may be absolute nonsense or quite legitimate. Even the fears that are nonsense have the potential to derail your plans, so always write them down. It's the first step in evaporating them.

It's your turn now – scribble your forces into the template in Exercise 4 or you can download a copy at corporateescapology. com/tools and play around.

Exercise 4: Forces Of Change

Exercise instructions

I recommend working clockwise round the model:

Step 1	Start with Pain. Identify three or four forces that are making you 'want out' of your Current World. They're usually pretty easy to find because they're the things you moan about to other people. The things that go round in your head on bad days.
Step 2	Project forward, what's attracting you to a New World? Feelings are fine at this stage – e.g. autonomy, freedom, purpose, etc. Or you can be more specific: I want to be a coach/retrain/build my own startup. Add three or four Progress forces.
Step 3	Next, jot down three or four Fears about that New World – is it predictable income, capability gaps, impact on family, a lack of self-confidence or clarity in what you could do?
Step 4	And finally, write down three or four Safety forces – things you're used to and rely on in your Current World – even if you know they're not necessarily good for you.
Step 5	Now you have populated the model, look objectively, is there enough combined strength from the sum of Pain and Progress to move you to exit, or are there too many frictions (Safety and Fear forces) holding you back?
	How could you reduce the drag of Safety and Fear forces to tip the balance in favour of Pain and Progress? Understanding the strength of these individual forces tells you about your state of readiness to exit.
Step 6	What do you notice about completing the model? Often it's easier to fill in what's making you want to move (Pain) than be crystal clear about what you're seeking from the change (Progress).

It's also often easier to write down our Fears about change than what we really value about staying put (Safety), which may be very little.

Notice where your energy lies when completing the model, what sparks your imagination?

Before this chapter closes, turn now to your Escape Plan Canvas in the Appendix and transpose a few of your thoughts into the boxes in the first column – what do you want in your new life, what is motivating you to change (the Pains and Progress forces) and what are the Fear forces holding you back?

Chapter summary

o   It's perfectly normal to look back (or look forward and imagine yourself looking back) and think 'What have I done?'. It doesn't mean you should go back.

o   Nostalgia does not give us 20/20 vision; it adds a rosy hue that filters out all the bad things – it was never really like that.

o   But just as it wasn't all good, it wasn't all bad either – and you will need to give up some things that you may value if you choose to leave.

o   Your identity and association with your company, or your role, are some of the things you will have to give up formally, although you will continue to be known for them long after you have left.

o   Rejection, whether you leave voluntarily or through a forced exit, is an inevitable feature of leaving and needs to be processed so it doesn't travel far with you after you've left.

o   Consciously understanding the forces that keep you locked to your Current World and pulled towards a New World is a useful method of building rational thinking about your state of readiness.

Forces Of Change

Pain

Current
world

Safety

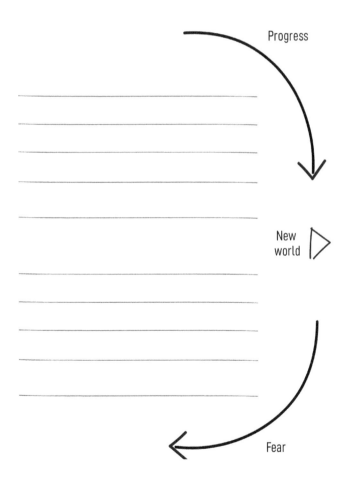

II Audit yourself

Part II of the Escape Method is about really getting to know yourself.

The complete you. Not the job title or the job descriptions, not the performance appraisals or the nice things people say when you've done a good bit of work. I'm talking about self-evaluation that's much deeper and broader.

Broader because it takes a cold, hard stare at who you really are, from a range of different perspectives, to describe a fuller, richer picture of what you can do and know – and how you could help others.

It's deeper because you will look at what constrains you, the red lines you can't or won't cross – and what drives you and why you're here. Both reading this book and on this planet.

Like an out-of-body experience where you get to see yourself as others do – and my guess is you're going to like it.

If Part I was about recognizing, more objectively, what you've given and gained from your corporate career, Part II is going to help you see the valuable person you've become.

CHAPTER 5

A genuine 360°

'Self-reverence, self-knowledge, self-control; these three alone lead life to sovereign power.'

Alfred, Lord Tennyson, Poet

Until now we've talked in generalities. Broad principles that explain what's going on – most people will relate to most of it.

But we're not interested in most people, we're interested in you. Unique, amazing and, likely, self-doubting you.

This chapter is an investment in understanding you, so you can see yourself the way others do.

Picture of you

Who are you, really?

You're probably the worst person to ask. Self-deprecation is likely to stop you from shouting your strengths from the rooftops. You'll probably come up with something bland, linked to your job title.

Like when Ricky Gervais in *The Office* (UK version) reviews Keith from Finance's development plan – he probes what Keith has put under strengths ('Accountancy'). It's funny, but it pretty well sums up a whole load of bad thinking we do about our strengths. If pressed, and we really need to be pressed, we can robotically list out bullets from our job description, which offers depressingly limited insights into who we are and what we can do.

Christy's story

Christy had worked for big pharmaceutical companies all her 26 years since graduating. She'd started off as a researcher, but quickly moved into commercial development roles which she found more interesting. She spent time in marketing, supply chain, policy, new markets and new product development over the years and in her early 50s, she felt she knew both a lot and also not very much.

Not very much that would be valuable in the outside world.

Christy's salary didn't match her expectations, which she put down to her lack of specialism and the way she'd moved around so much inside her last company. She felt trapped by her current employer – but didn't dare risk leaving and finding herself without a role.

When I met Christy and asked her to tell me about her experience, she reeled off a list of job titles. When I asked about her skills, she came up with just three. When I asked what she was good at, she clammed up completely.

Christy's problem was that she hadn't forensically evaluated her skills, experiences and knowledge in so long, if ever, that she had stopped valuing her offer and contribution.

She was not in the right place to start looking for another job; she had low confidence and self-belief, because she didn't really know herself or the value she brought others. She defaulted to the generics: 'I'm a good team player', 'I'm the one that organizes the social events', 'I'm the one who takes new people under my wing'.

All quite laudable, but not, it transpired, Christy's big strengths.

Through some of my exercises, Christy realized she was actually terrific at marketing and communications, especially in more technical fields, drawing on her background.

Once Christy understood this – and had these skills validated by colleagues, previous bosses and external contacts – she began to look for a new job with renewed confidence. But she didn't find one – instead, she resigned and set up as a marketing freelancer, partnering with a friend who had complementary graphic design skills.

I must have been in my late 30s when someone pointed me to Gallup's StrengthFinder®. There was a line in the book about wasting time trying to improve weaknesses at the expense of improving, and capitalizing on, our strengths. All through education I'd unconsciously tried to become average-to-good at everything, instead of amazing at just a few differentiating things people valued and that I enjoyed.

I work with lots of startups today and I tell them the same thing I'll tell you: focus on the sweet spot between what you're good at (and enjoy), what creates value for others and what sets you apart.

Building an objective 360° profile

What you are going to do now is develop the kind of description you really wish your line manager would write about you – or how you hope people talk about you when you aren't there.

It's going to be entirely accurate and honest. Moreover, it will lack the self-deprecation and self-censoring you would typically do to avoid embarrassment, because from now on you're only interested in describing your very best self.

You're going to start with some data gathering. You need good source material from which to build your 360° profile.

I've developed three exercises to help you delve deep into all your past experiences to draw out what you do best:

1   Six Shoes.

2   Best Of Times, Worst Of Times.

3   Six Prisms.

But first I want you to look in your folders to dig out any personality or psychometric tests that you've completed over the years: Myers-Briggs Type Indicator®, Insights Discovery®, Gallup's StrengthFinder®, FIRO-B® and anything else. Also, grab your CV, even if it's a bit dusty, any performance reviews, particularly in years where you thrived – and any emails where you were given feedback from others.

You don't need to do anything with them yet – they are your source material.

Now let's start with the exercises. Don't overthink them, you're just trying to uncover interesting things about you. Don't simplify the data or try to synthesize them in any way, keep them raw.

I'll show you what to do with everything you capture in a few pages time.

1. Six Shoes

It's an evolution of Edward de Bono's Six Thinking Hats, where each person in a meeting takes on a specific perspective to really challenge an idea or decision: The White Hat wants facts, The Black Hat sees risks, The Yellow Hat's optimistic, etc.

What you need to do is step into six different shoes of six different people and evaluate yourself. What would each say that you do really well. Forget what they'd say about your weaknesses.

1   Manager shoe: pick a boss that you've enjoyed working with. One who was grateful, ideally one who couldn't do what you can do and wasn't threatened by that. How would your manager describe you to a peer or their boss?

2   Coach shoe: even when they challenge you, your coach is on your side, and they bring objectivity to help you recognize your strengths and the progress you've made. How would they describe you (anonymously) to inspire another client?

3   Customer shoe: it could be an internal or external customer, someone you've helped or for whom you've solved a problem. How do they describe you and the lengths to which you've gone to make them happy and satisfied?

4   Head-hunter shoe: the recruiter you engaged a few months back when you thought that jumping to another corporate ship was your only option. He's paid to sing your praises, talk you up, embellish the facts, really sell you. Listen to him for a bit while he sells you to a client, then write down what he says.

5   Colleague shoe: think of a time when someone appeared at your desk, came up to you at a school or community event, emailed you from out of the blue – what do they see in you that made them ask for help? Was it your knowledge or the way you use that knowledge? Was it something about the kind of person you are and reputation you have?

6   Friend shoe: pick a good friend, one who sees the real you – who may have already noticed that you're ready for something new, who may have recognized your untapped potential, who's cheerleading you from the side. What do they see unencumbered by your inner critic?

Now fill in the table in Exercise 5 – don't be shy. Remember it's other people saying this about you, so you can drop any awkwardness.

Exercise 5: Six Shoes

Exercise instructions

Step 1	Turn on your empathy switch and step into each set of shoes – how do they see you, what are the things they see you excel at, your unique contribution, the reason they want you on their team helping to solve problems and making the world a better place?
Step 2	Jot down a few bullets under each shoe and then take a step back. What common themes do you see? Are the same descriptions of how you work, help others and problem-solve coming up?

Six Shoes

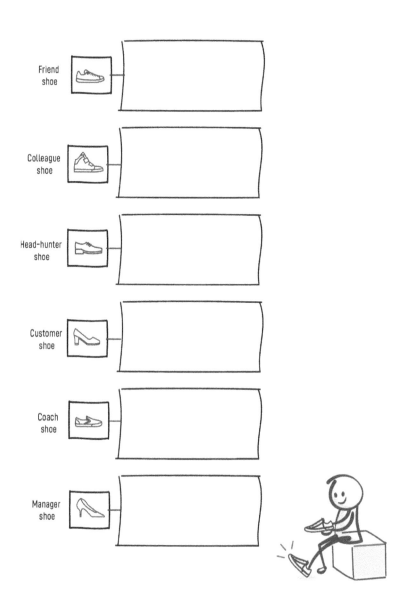

2. *Best Of Times, Worst Of Times*
The second exercise is about pushing you to think in extremes. Our corporate lives are often a classic bell curve with the routine stuff filling >90% of the time.

The remainder goes horrendously wrong (and you fix it) or it's utterly amazing (because of you). This is what we become famous for.

The routine stuff won't help much here because it doesn't differentiate you outside – or inside for that matter. It's the stuff that helps you shine that we're interested in.

I learnt probably my most valuable lesson a year into my consulting job. I was working for the UK Cabinet Office and had invited all the CEOs of the giant media companies in the UK for a meeting about Digital TV policy (I am that old). A month before the meeting we changed the date. I informed all the people who had accepted, but not the ones who hadn't.

They found out when they climbed four flights to a venue on the wrong side of Westminster on the wrong date. I'd taken that day off and I was in the shower, blissfully ignorant – until I checked my voicemail. Or rather a series of increasingly angry voicemails.

I didn't last long working for that client.

But before I left, I wrote apologies to every single person and I put checks in place to make sure they came to the rescheduled event.

That episode taught me that while I am terrible at detail, at tasks that require a really methodical mind, I clean up my mess, I'm a fixer.

I can think of four or five things that made me famous in BP, that went much better than I could ever have dreamt and which I lived off in terms of reputation for years. Underpinning these successes were common strengths or skills I drew on that made me stand out: instinct for customer, empathy, creativity, respect for technical detail, breaking rules.

Now it's your turn (see Exercise 6).

Best Of Times, Worst Of Times

Best of times   Worst of times

Exercise 6: Best Of Times, Worst Of Times

Exercise instructions

Step 1 Shut yourself away and close your eyes. Think back to a time when you were *on fire* (not literally). When you were knocking it out the park. You know, the time when everyone was smiling, wanting you to be part of their team, when you felt really good – what were you doing, what skills and know-how were you demonstrating, what made you feel so good? Add some bullets into the left-hand box.

Step 2 And then, think about the big screw-ups, the times when everything seemed to be going wrong, when it felt like it was just you left to sort things – what did you do, how did you approach the problem, how did you motivate others to help, what did you learn?

Jot down notes in the right-hand box.

Step 3	What do you notice between these two sets of bullets – are there any consistent themes in your approach, the strengths on which you drew, how you were viewed by others?

3. Six Prisms

For the third exercise of this 360° profiling work, I want you to capture as broad a picture as possible of where your strengths lie as an expert in corporate life.

This is important for two reasons:

1 Many of the things we do in corporate life we assume anyone can do (but they can't).

2 We forget we've learnt how to do these things and are often unconscious of them because we've been doing them for so long.

In my experience, these are often tremendous sources of value to others. They're the things that help you deliver value fast, and almost immediately, with minimal guidance or training. They're the things that make you reliable because you can see the risks and you can pre-empt issues. They're the things that mean you know what 'good' looks like and they're the things that drive efficiency.

I've said before I'm always staggered and a little bit sad when I talk to corporate people, often senior leaders, who doubt whether someone else, e.g. a startup founder, would want to talk to them, or receive mentoring or listen to them talk on stage or on a podcast.

It's the dint of repetition, if you do something long enough you stop valuing it – because you assume no-one else does.

This exercise looks at you through six prisms of corporate instinct. The things you can do that others have never learnt to do; the things you've spent years getting so good at, that you've forgotten there are other inferior ways.

1 **Strategy**: You don't have to have worked in corporate strategy to think strategically. Not if you've spent time working in a corporate. You simply can't get your projects or budgets approved without demonstrating a link to strategy.

Corporate people look for context, frameworks, patterns that make them and their work relevant and aligned. Internal Communications leads the way, with the CEO townhalls and webcasts, followed by leaders lower down in the organization robotically spinning the latest vernacular and 10-point plans. Pretty quickly everyone gets with the programme.

Common strategic skills: Defining context, Sharing context, Competitor landscaping, Strategy development, Analysis, Reporting, Business case development, Media analysis, Budget preparation & presentation.

2   **Stakeholders**: Because no person in a corporate is an island or omnipotent, everyone quickly learns to appreciate the significance of stakeholders in decision-making and influence. Your role only exists because a group of stakeholders agreed that it was required. Working in a corporate is a bit like walking around accompanied by an invisible network where some people hold you back, other people propel you forward, some try to trip you up, others lend you their wings. The ability to identify, understand and manage stakeholders is a hugely undervalued skill that fast becomes an instinct. Survival of the fittest kicks in for those who don't evolve fast enough.

Common stakeholder skills: Stakeholder mapping, Chairing meetings, Representing others, Effective delegation, Empathy, Active listening, Coaching, Communications, Negotiation, Influencing, Contracting, Briefing, Synthesising, Sales, Marketing, Chief of Staff, Presenting, Team leadership.

3   **Quality**: Corporates' products, whether tangible like a bubble bath or motor vehicle, or intangible like a report or brand, have to meet the highest standards of public scrutiny, often legal or regulatory. This emphasis on quality percolates through the organization, so when someone sees a poorly put-together slide-deck or a document with typos, the company logo stretched or a jarring tone of voice, it's noted. You probably know how to correct it. You quickly learn in corporate life that 'good enough' is rarely acceptable in a corporate – 'perfection' is almost always better than 'done' (hence the glacial pace). There are

consequences for poor attention to quality and there are also big advantages for those who hit the bar every time.

Common quality skills: Design, Product, Proof-reading, Attention to detail, Brand, Communications, Investor relations, Socializing ideas, Feedback, Quality assurance.

4   **Risk**: This is the uber-prism – it transcends everything for corporate people. So much of what we do in our jobs is about managing and mitigating risk: reputational, financial, safety, people, cyber-security, compliance. Your nose for risk develops pretty quickly in a corporate – as ideas that would be cheered from the rafters in a smaller organization (and trialled that week) are frowned on or crushed with condescension in a big company culture (often without any evidence). 'No' is always easier than 'Yes' in a corporate. But it's not (always) all about risk elimination; managing risk is a valuable skill indeed that corporate people learn fast.

Common risk skills: Risk quantification, Scenario planning, Risk mitigation, Risk communication, Auditing, Risk workshopping, Training, Certification, Safety walkthroughs, Emergency response, Contingency planning, After actions reviews, Capturing lessons learnt.

5   **Impact**: Corporate people also develop a good radar for impact, however it may be measured. Results, results, results. Whole teams exist to measure impact and performance with everyone working around them to feed the machine. Corporate people are also good at scrutinizing whether something delivers impact, which option delivers most bang for your buck, how many X for Y? And if the leading indicators of impact aren't immediately obvious, hackles start to rise.

Common impact skills: Business case development, Assurance, Performance management, Portfolio management, Finance, Social performance, Corporate social responsibility, Reporting, Investor relations, Strategy, Testing, Prototyping.

6   **Sustain or Scale**: Repeatability is key to creating value in a corporate; very little has impact if it's one-off. When something is successfully delivered once, it generally needs to be shared and executed by different teams, businesses,

markets, geographies, etc. Corporate people get good at standardizing, productizing, proceduralizing and optimizing. Entire departments exist to develop and enforce common standards, group practices and rules. The mantra 'continuous improvement' is the hallmark of any corporate worth its salt.

Common sustain/scale skills: Process development, Systems design, How-to guides, checklists & templates, Knowledge management, Best practice, Continuous improvement, Training course design, Training delivery, Change management, Project/Programme management, Records management.

Now you've understood the six prisms, it's time to look through them to see the real you (see Exercise 7). If writing in books is not your thing, you'll find all the exercises and templates free to download at corporateescapology.com/tools.

Exercise 7: Six Prisms

Exercise instructions

I want you to walk through each prism and think whether you have skills, experience or knowledge acquired through your corporate jobs that make up who you are today – and the offer and contribution you make to those around you.

Look especially hard where you're using skills and knowledge quite unconsciously to get things done. The common skills listed previously should help dredge your memory for examples.

Step 1	Strategy doesn't necessarily mean you've worked in a strategy team – it's how you bring in context and how you identify the steps of getting from A to B.
Step 2	Stakeholders can be internal to get your projects moving or when working cross-functionally, or externally if you have customers or industry partners you need to engage.
Step 3	Quality can refer to the checks and assurances you put in place before you email a document, just as much as it refers to perfecting your company's product before market.

Step 4 You don't have to work in Risk to have questioned the probability and impact of something happening and to have tried to communicate it to others.

Step 5 Impact is how you seek to both measure and manage outcomes.

Step 6 Sustain or Scale relates to how you take a one-off deliverable, maybe even a pilot, and make it more robust, optimized and available to others.

Six Prisms

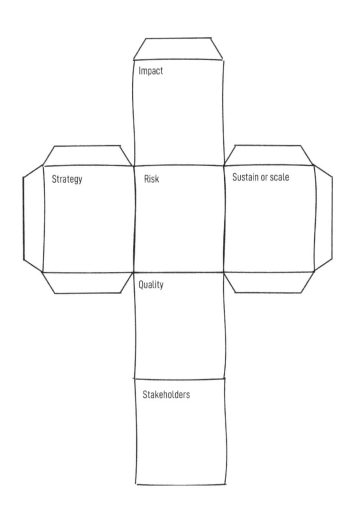

I'm sure you identified with many of these common skills, even if your role wasn't formally in any of these functions. Collectively, they make up the lion's share of most corporate jobs – whether it's how we're conducting ourselves in a workshop, a document we're producing, an event we're running, a customer visit, rolling out a new system, onboarding a new hire or interviewing one.

The last three exercises have hopefully made you feel pretty good. I always feel like preparing for an interview is good on the ego because you get to focus only on your brilliance (and you only need to admit one weakness – that turns out to be a hidden strength). So, wallow in this for a bit. Your current situation may not be making you very happy right now, but you've turned a corner through Part I getting into the right mindset and this chapter should have helped you see that you have a really wide range of things you're actually very good at – and are therefore likely to be valued by others.

There's one more thing you can do at this point. To avoid the risk that you've been a little too self-deprecating about what you can do – or that you've missed something that others see that you don't or don't value about yourself – show these pages to a friend or colleague that you trust and see if they see anything you've missed.

People like to help. They also like to say nice things. A long list is better at this point – and if you don't agree with something you can always drop it later.

Sense-making

Now it's time to make sense out of your seemingly disparate data. This is one of my skill areas, probably one of the few things I gained from my history degree. I instinctively see patterns and themes in everything I come across. And I can do it really fast.

This is one of those classic skills, honed over years, decades, that I would never write in a CV or even necessarily think about in an interview. Unless the job specifically demanded it. And yet, it's a skill I draw on every week, possibly every day.

It's one of the unconscious skills that I developed and mastered in my corporate roles and now package up and offer to other people.

That's one of mine. And you're now going to find some of yours.

Some of you may look at this kind of task with apprehension and even fear. What will lighten the fear a little is the fact that we're going to make sense of a lot of wonderful things about you. What could be nicer? It's like having your best friend talk about all the reasons they like, admire and value you.

A word about your mindset at this point. You have to be in the right place to do this well. If you're not feeling positive or optimistic, put this exercise off until you are. A good way to test your mood is to smile. If ten seconds later you're still smiling you're good to go; if the smile fades within ten seconds, put it off and deal with whatever's obviously more pressing. But don't skip it, or you're unlikely to build the confidence in yourself to move – because you won't have built your supporting evidence.

There are six steps to sense-making:

> 1) Prepare -> 2) Select -> 3) Cluster -> 4) Rest, recover & revisit ->
> 5) Write-up -> 6) Reflect.

You need a decent couple of hours to do this. Do not fit it into an hour between Teams calls. It's too important to rush. If you don't get the right mindset from Part I and your unique offer from Part II, you'll be unprepared for the leap and put your new future at risk.

This is me being serious.

But on this I am. Don't read this in bed on your Kindle and think 'I'll just do this in my head'. Been there. Don't make this book one of those books.

Step 1 – Prepare
Surround yourself with the sources of data from your psychometric tests, CV (no matter how out of date), old performance reviews, emails with feedback and, of course, your newly completed templates from the last three exercises.

The best thing I can recommend at this point to keep things really open is to use different coloured sticky notes. Writing in a book, or even in a Word document or Google sheet, makes things very linear and for this exercise you need the freedom of moving things around – trying things out, finding you're wrong and retracing your steps. Miro and other tools, like Jamboard and even Trello, can help because they both have the dynamic functionality you need for this task.

To give your preparation a bit of structure I recommend grouping your data into five categories:

1 Skills – the things you've learnt to do.

2 Experiences – the jobs and tasks you've accomplished.

3 Knowledge – what you know.

4 Strengths – your natural abilities (that you've polished).

5 Energizers – the things that get you in flow.

It helpfully creates the acronym SEKSE.

Your SEKSE.

Or, if you like, You're SEKSE.

You can use five different sheets of paper, but sticky notes on a wall is a thing of beauty. Pick a colour for each category. Find a wall that you can keep free for a day or two for your stickies. This is an important investment in you – like a corporate might do when planning a new strategy or market move.

Step 2 – Select

Scan through each source and pick out keywords that jump out at you. Write the keyword in capitals on the coloured sticky note that best fits the SEKSE category – and see if you can add a line of explanation or an example in lower case underneath. Then move to the next source and pick out more, noticing a concentration of the same keywords coming up.

Step 3 – Cluster
After you've worked through a couple of data sources, stop and look at your sticky notes – do you notice any common themes you can cluster? You're not wedded to these clusters, they may be wrong – but they're hypotheses and more data will prove or disprove them.

Now go back to your source material and keep adding the sticky notes until you've gone through everything.

Step 4 – Rest, recover & revisit
Probably a good point to get a cup of tea now. Have a break.

Even better, come back to this the following day.

But before you do, get a photo or several. Just in case an annoying person removes the sticky notes or they fall off the wall. Or you get busy and distracted.

I would love to see them and am happy to make a few observations and probe a bit – send me a photo on Instagram @ corporateescapologist or by email to adam@corporateescapology. com.

It's good to sleep on this or at least have some time away from the wall to avoid becoming a bit incremental in your thinking. Also, it's tiring and becomes easier to force-fit the sticky notes to existing groups because they 'sort of go with each other', when actually they're different and potentially of interest to explore further.

When you go back fresh, look carefully at each sticky note for a moment or two to:

1   reassure yourself you've not missed anything.

2   confirm it's in the right cluster – if it could fit in more than one cluster create more than one sticky note.

3   check it doesn't need to be more granular because it's written at too high a level.

OK, now stand back. What do you think? How does it make you feel?

It should give you a warm glow and an increase in confidence because you have an interesting mix of skills, experience and knowledge — as well as the evidence that proves it.

If you aren't feeling this warm glow, and I was coaching you, I would probably ask if you thought you needed to do the exercise again.

Which would be my way of telling you to do the exercise again. Properly this time.

Step 5 – Write it up

I always hate it in workshops when a lazy facilitator sends out photos of the sticky notes as if that's in any way a summary. You have to write it up. And add value. So that's our next job (see Exercise 8).

Exercise 8: You're SEKSE And You Know It

Exercise instructions

Step 1	Look at your wall of sticky notes (or your papers) and for each SEKSE category, write your top five in the following template. Pick the things that stand out to you and also the things you like best.
Step 2	Star any that you really think set you apart and where you add most value.

Don't over-work this. Perfection is the enemy of done. In my experience, you can't help but tinker with it over the next few days and weeks anyway, so don't waste your time now. Just write it up.

You're SEKSE And You Know It

	1	2	3	4	5
Skills The things you've learnt to do					

	1	2	3	4	5
Experience The jobs and tasks you've done					

	1	2	3	4	5
Know-how The stuff you've learnt					

	1	2	3	4	5
Strengths Your natural abilities (that you've polished)					

	1	2	3	4	5
Energizers The things that get you in 'flow'					

Step 6 – Reflect
As I say, there's more refining you can do with this, but let's end this exercise with an attempt at some objective observation of what you've written down.

o   What have you noticed?

o   Any new capabilities that surprised you?

o   Any capabilities that had more supporting evidence than others?

o   Any changes compared with other times you've done similar exercises?

o   Any capabilities you feel you need to explore further?

o   Were there more capabilities than you expected – or fewer?

o   How do you feel about your capabilities?

o   How many of your capabilities are limited to a corporate job, to your corporate job, or could be relevant and valued in other settings?

Now, be brave and share this with a few people – some people you trust, ideally ones who will be honest with you. More often than not they see different things you'll miss. They will usually be much more positive about you than you are about yourself, so listen. But seek out evidence – ask them when they saw that capability demonstrated.

If there's evidence for what they see, add it in. Especially if you hear the same thing from other people. Be pragmatic. Just because it wasn't on the sticky note board, you can still add it on. You're not in a corporate workshop now.

That's it. I hope you now have a pretty amazing 360° profile, with the evidence to build confidence in your valuable offer and the self-belief to give it a try.

This chapter has hopefully helped you see the bigger you. The one that other people see – and will increasingly see as you exit your corporate job.

'Wealth of experience' may be a cliché, but it's what you have been building throughout your corporate career and it's what will create new wealth for you now – whatever wealth means to you – in your next chapter.

Don't feel bad if you're planning to walk out taking that 'wealth' with you – you've returned that value over the years to the companies who hired you. It's perfectly legitimate and perfectly fair.

Chapter summary

o   Humans tend to be quite incremental, rarely stepping back and evaluating their growth, progress and achievements.

o   Self-awareness is key to building the confidence to explore options outside of your corporate career and to identify how your skills, experiences and know-how can be deployed to create value for others.

o   This kind of audit can even help if you choose not to leave.

o   Evaluating yourself objectively is challenging but possible by expanding the data sources used for self-evaluation – psychometric profiling, performance reviews, informal feedback and probing deeply into past experiences.

o   Because corporate people are surrounded by corporate people, they have a tendency not to recognize or value some of their capabilities, because they believe everyone has them.

o   This is not the time to be self-effacing about your skills, experiences and know-how – one way to help is to imagine you are evaluating a friend you love and support. You will be less judgemental, look for positives and recognize more success.

o   Once you have summarized your self-evaluation, do the brave thing and share it with a range of people – they may see you differently, surface things you've missed and can provide evidence to support your hypotheses.

CHAPTER 6

What's holding you back?

'The more constraints one imposes, the more one frees one's self. And the arbitrariness of the constraint serves only to obtain precision of execution.'

Igor Stravinsky, Composer

I hoped you tried to keep positive and optimistic about yourself in the last chapter because this one is 'a bit dark'. Temporarily at least. It's where we probe a bit more into your fears, both rational and irrational, and the harsh realities with which you'll need to deal before moving on.

I'm a glass half full kind of person. I'm pretty confident that a decision usually works out for the best and a change is always (eventually) positive. But when it comes to leaving a corporate job, I'm more circumspect, because the risks are higher.

But you don't need to take them all at the same time.

Going into a whole-of-life disruption without proper preparation is reckless – especially if you have responsibilities, which you'll likely have if you're some way into your career.

Corporate Escapology is about getting prepared, with the right mindset from Part I and emerging clarity about your capabilities from the last chapter. But it's also about being realistic about some of the constraints, the red lines and boundaries that exist for you – and that may exist for others around you.

The financial reality

I'm not sure anyone thinks about leaving corporate life without questioning its affordability. It's probably the first thing most of you will think about. And that is a good thing, because the inability to afford your life on the other side is likely to be the single biggest reason you will fail or need to jump back into a corporate job.

There are usually three aspects of losing a salary which hurt when you leave:

o   The amount, which tends to be quite good, compared with many other jobs.

o   The frequency, which tends to be monthly, like many of your significant outgoings.

o   The predictability with which it arrives in your account, usually on the day you expect.

The last point is possibly the most important of all. Much of life revolves around having a regular income, more in fact than the amount in absolute terms. Arranging a credit agreement for my smart watch through my health insurance was more challenging without a regular salary, even though the amount was small. Big things, like leasing a car, and even bigger things, like mortgages, can be problematic.

A salary still counts for something as many self-employed people will testify – things are a bit more challenging without 'proof of income' which usually means payslips for the last three months.

It's absurd, of course, because that salary can come to a grinding halt in month four; the past isn't always a very good predictor of the future. Most corporate jobs today provide only one to three months' notice which, if you think about it, doesn't give that much comfort if you have commitments that extend into the future.

I remember the first day after I left my job, when my salary would have ordinarily come in and it didn't because I was no longer employed. I noticed it because all I saw was the haemorrhaging of cash due to the direct debits which had nothing to draw down against and I went horribly overdrawn. I quickly learnt the lesson that it was up to me to provide the income to afford the costs. The Salary Fairy had flown away.

Most of you will have a lot of fixed costs by the time you're ready to leave. That may be mortgage or rent, cars, children, school or university fees, as well all the minutiae of utilities, insurances and the seemingly endless subscription services.

On top of this you may have a certain lifestyle expectation, including holidays and weekends away, eating out, clothes, exercise classes, coffees, cleaners, etc., which can feel less and less discretionary, even if they're really not. I personally have an unhealthy obsession with plants (especially ones with yellow reduced labels crying out to be rescued). Reining-in that spending takes self-discipline.

Other benefits

Salary is the big one of course, but there are other benefits often provided as part of your package. I'm talking here about car allowances, medical cover, life insurance and, another big one, pensions. If you want to continue getting access to these things you'll have to front up the (post-tax) cash for them.

You may also receive share options or have access to share schemes through your employer. I was using dividends from my share options to build a savings pot and had forgotten this when I planned my exit, meaning I was short of the cash after I had left. This was one of my oversights when planning my exit, because I'd not looked at every line of income and expenditure.

You might also receive an annual bonus. In the year I left, the company cancelled our bonus as a nod to the thousands of people it was making redundant, but before then it was as reliable as clockwork. It usually paid for our holiday, work on the house, as well as paying off a bit of overdraft that had accrued over the year. If we wanted the holiday and the house renovations to continue, I had to find cash for these things (and stop going into my overdraft).

It's not the most fun work, unless you love spreadsheets and budgeting, but it's important to build a complete picture of your finances to avoid unpleasant surprises down the track.

Other constraints

There are also other non-financial constraints which need factoring into the decision to leave, or, at the very least, the timing of your exit.

Childcare – if you're incredibly fortunate it may be on offer at your workplace. Some corporates help fund childcare or make it easy to access tax benefits. But even if you don't have direct childcare benefits from your employer, you may have an arrangement that could be disrupted by a change of employer and lifestyle.

Qualifications – maybe your company is supporting you to gain a qualification, e.g. through continuous professional development or even time off. They may have imposed restrictions on when you can leave.

Promotion – you may be in line for a promotion, which, if secured, might add more to your credentials or create new opportunities. Waiting a few months might add more value to your offer afterwards.

Moving house or re-mortgaging – if you are planning to move home or need access to any significant credit, you may want to consider deferring any move – and only after you've reassured yourself that any new obligations are affordable for your new life.

Having a baby – having children is hard enough without the financial pressure of losing an income. Corporates (especially in the UK and Europe) tend to be pretty generous with maternity leave and, increasingly, with paternity leave. Think carefully before leaving if you plan to build or extend your family.

Health concerns – I hate the idea of staying somewhere just to access future benefits. I worked with many people who were quite open about disliking the job but only 'staying for the pension'. It feels like a half-life to me, but I'll try not to judge.

But when it comes to health, I feel a bit differently. Unless you're very unhappy, if you have health concerns, you may be better off sticking with the stability of your corporate job, until you're ready.

Whilst it's reckless to leave your corporate job without considering its financial implications, it's also important not to overstate the risks, or imagine you are more dependent than you really are. Like the 360° profiling of the last chapter, a forensic audit of your financial position could help build a more objective assessment whether the risks are too high or can be managed or mitigated.

It's quite common for people to justify staying put based on old assumptions around financial obligations and constraints.

Exercise 9 might help, but I'm no financial advisor; seek professional advice before you exit.

Exercise 9: Reality Check

Exercise instructions

Step 1	For each of the main financial dependencies – salary, bonus, other benefits, other constraints – mark High, Medium or Low.
Step 2	Use the following boxes to get more specific about the dependency, e.g. you're likely to need the salary to pay your mortgage or rent. But why are you dependent on your bonus? What could you not do if it ended? Which benefits do you truly depend on – healthcare, pension, insurance?
Step 3	For each dependency identify at least one way you might mitigate it by doing something different (even if you don't know how just yet).
	For example, you could potentially mitigate your current salary if you had a three or four month buffer. You could lessen your dependency on an annual bonus by going on a cheaper holiday – or no holiday. You could pay your own health insurance or finish paying for a qualification yourself.

Step 4   The next step is to add a Confidence factor (High/ Medium/Low) for each of your potential mitigations. For instance, you might feel Low confidence in your ability to build a buffer, if you don't believe you will earn any income for six months. This might then force you to find an alternative mitigation, e.g. seek part-time contract work to build a buffer. You may feel Medium confidence in that.

Step 5   The final step is to reflect on the table – are these constraints real or imagined, are some excuses? Do some of your mitigations address more than one constraint?

Reality Check

	Dependencies			
	on salary	on bonus	on other benefits	on other constraints
Extent of dependency				
Get specific				
Potential mitigations				
Confidence in mitigations				

Get prepared

The first practical thing you need to do is understand what it costs to live the way you want to live. For most of us that will mean looking back over a typical month, or even better a few, to see how you spend your lovely salary.

It's pretty depressing work I know, unless you live like a monk. What we think we spend tends to be lower than what we actually spend.

One thing I noticed in myself, and I have observed in many others, is that because we don't really enjoy our jobs, we treat ourselves a lot outside of work.

One of the most harrowing accounts of this behaviour I read about was Brooke Taylor's, now a coach and corporate trainer in what she called *The Success Wound*. I first heard Brooke on my friend Erica D'Eramo's podcast. Brooke was like many corporate people, a high achiever right through school, college and into work. She was clever, resourceful and she worked like a demon. By the weekend she was utterly burnt out – so she partied to recover, which sadly led to alcohol addiction.

Her story is extreme, but resonated with me because throughout her life she fed on the external validation of teachers, exam results, job offers, hitting company objectives, promotions, etc. Many corporate people are like this. I was. And if you step back far enough, companies aren't that different from schools in many respects: the head teacher, the teachers, the structure, the rules, the hard work = results, the successes, the failures.

As Steve Cook, one of my podcast guests, said, 'They (Corporates) kind of turn you into a bit of a child because you become what you're taught to be... and you always have to seek their approval. In many ways it's like being in school.'

And as anyone with teenagers can testify, they want to blow out at the weekend.

Many adults are the same – with more constraints but also more available cash. It's human nature to live to our means – and, for many people, well beyond them.

The new you is likely to have more constraints without a regular salary coming in, it's true. But you will also have more opportunities to enjoy what you do and feel less like you need to reward yourself for putting up with a job that you don't enjoy.

Breaking free from a corporate will give you the opportunity to reset things because of this. Begin with a cold, hard look at your lifestyle and what it costs.

Firstly, I will admit that I hate budgets. I had five years in finance, doing planning and performance management, and I loathed it. I view it as my wilderness period.

I hate working on a home budget just as much. But the thought of it is always a whole heap worse than actually doing it.

So get on and build one. You owe it to yourself and to the others around you. It will highlight where you are spending wisely and where you are wasting money, enabling you to make different choices when you've made the move.

I haven't added an exercise here as you're not going to work up a thorough budget in a book – and it's confidential. There's great software that can help you do this – sometimes linked to your bank for actual spend.

The key is to be realistic when budgeting. If you always had an annual summer holiday and will feel bad if you have to cut it after you've left your job, then plan for it. But without the bonus to help finance it, you will have to find the funds somewhere else. Same for the Friday night takeaway or the summer wardrobe.

Most of the work budgets I built in my job I never looked at again until the end of the year when I realized I'd overspent (only to be rescued by everyone else who had underspent). It was pretty irresponsible. I'm less like that now. I know what I've got to spend and most months I check how well I did – to identify if I need a top-up for some unforeseen one-offs or if I need to change a bad behaviour.

The budget review is important because you won't have that luxury of the annual bonus or share options to come to your rescue – so you need to keep a tight rein on spending.

My wife, Megan, never asked to see the budget I built which proved I could leave BP, but I subjected her to a budget review every month for the first year to reassure her that we were spending in line with our plan and we looked ok for the next month. Eventually we stopped because life is too short and we find it hard enough to get time together without wasting what we do have poring over Excel. But only now, years after my exit.

Buffering

I have already come clean that in spite of a terrific salary, bonus and benefits, each year I had to raid some savings to clear the overdraft. It's depressingly common so I don't feel too bad and nor should you. But it can't continue when you're working for yourself or have an irregular income.

You need a buffer. This has been the big regulator since I left my corporate job. Having a pot of cash that gives me six months' backup in the event of the sky falling in. When I was paid a salary I never had a buffer – we dipped into the overdraft, occasionally using a credit card, raiding the school fees fund if we had an unexpected cost, the boiler, a leak, something medical, etc.

Another of my podcast guests, Katie Tucker, told me, 'A buffer is the secret to not panicking'.

I couldn't agree more. I've coached people who have left their corporate jobs and focused on building a sales pipeline for their consulting businesses and they are stressed – because they have limited influence over that sales pipeline. A buffer lies within your circle of control and, unlike a pipeline, it is cold hard cash.

It may take time to build, but a buffer is the post-corporate equivalent of your salary; it quietens some of the anxiety generated by personal responsibility.

Unconstrained potential

You may not be wanting to leave just to make more money – there's likely to be something deeper. But cash flow is a pre-requisite when you have responsibilities, so it needs careful thought and planning.

That said, moving out of corporate life presents you with an opportunity to make more money.

Right now in your corporate job your capacity for earning is restricted to what your one company chooses to pay you. You can work 40 hours a week or 80 and you get paid the same. You can work every weekend and see nothing extra for it, other than burnout and resentment.

Whereas working for yourself means, in theory, you can get paid more fairly for the work you do. If you need a bit extra this month, you can potentially take on more work. This is over-simplistic of course, but you get the point. Your earning capacity is no longer constrained by your employer. And that's quite exciting – and can make you feel more secure than you did when employed.

It's like Emma Gannon says harnessing versatility in her book on portfolio careers, The Multi-Hyphen Method, 'I feel much more secure and confident knowing that by having multiple skills I have a diverse digital CV and I'm more employable'.

So, let's end the money section here. The financials are the deal-breaker for most people wanting to exit corporate life. They matter, it's naïve to deny it, but they don't need to control the decision. With careful planning, budgeting and a buffer, as well as the right interventions on your costs, a viable income stream (or multiple streams) and a regular review to make sure that you're on track, you can manage your finances to sustain your new life.

Stakeholder management

There may be people around you who aren't quite so enthusiastic about your plans to walk away from the corporate cash cow. My wife, Megan, was wary to say the least. She thought I deserved to leave, but she found it hugely destabilizing.

She was herself a corporate player at Marks & Spencer, a lingerie buyer, earning more money than me when we first met. She gave it up, and her London life, to move with me to Aberdeenshire, 40 miles from the nearest town, which was definitely not London. And we started a family.

Megan is very entrepreneurial and over the years has run several businesses. She is a very successful upholsterer, which she does from her workshop at home, but she had agreed to be the primary carer while the children were young.

So, when I said I wanted to volunteer for redundancy, with all its associated uncertainties, she very naturally felt insecure. She actually said, 'that wasn't what I'd signed up for'.

Corporate people learn the art of stakeholder management pretty quickly working in big companies. It's a matter of survival (of self, as much as of ideas and projects).

But even if you're a consummate diplomat at work, you may not always apply the same rigour with your most important stakeholders, your family.

You may not take time before announcing a thought or a decision which could affect them (in this case disrupt them fundamentally). You may not think through how they might feel, why they might feel like this, what information they need, where the opportunities or benefits lie for them.

You might come home and say, 'They're making redundancies at work (again), I think I might lose my job', without really thinking how your family might take the news. You may have processed all your angst on the way home.

I announced my idea to leave in quite a cavalier way over dinner. In my mind it was a brainstorm, for which I was looking for (positive) feedback and reaction. In Megan's it was like the ground had suddenly opened up.

Don't do what I did. Think about your partner.

We did better with the children, through luck rather than good stakeholder planning. We took them for lunch at RHS Wisley and said we had something important to talk to them about. The sheer relief on their faces when they found out we weren't getting a divorce showed that me leaving my job was low on their list of worries.

My mum had died the previous year, which was, in this particular case, a relief as I'm sure she'd have felt like Megan. My dad talked positively about his own enforced escape from corporate life, setting up business as a yacht charterer, so he was fine.

Telling Megan's parents was a bit more of a challenge, but by then Megan was more reconciled (I think supportive would probably be an overstatement). So she could allay any of their concerns better than I could.

The primary concern people have whenever faced with someone exiting their job is the risk to stable cash flow.

But there may be other stakeholders in your decision to leave your steady income. Maybe there are people or organizations to whom you owe money.

And not just financial stakeholders – there may be people relying on you: people you mentor, people counting on you for a promotion, people who expected you to be their successor. You may have agreed to speak at a conference or help someone out and your exit may impact them.

List these things (see Exercise 10) and think through how each of your stakeholders might feel, so you manage them appropriately – with minimal surprises. This is something you will instinctively do – or formally do – in your corporate job, so just use the same approach in your private life to help ease your transition.

If you need more space for your notes, all the exercises and templates are free to download at corporateescapology.com/tools.

Exercise 10: *Stakeholder Mapping*

Exercise instructions

Step 1	For each oval in the template, add the name of a stakeholder in your decision to exit corporate life.
Step 2	In each box behind the oval, write down the position you expect them to take, e.g. resistant, supportive, negative, positive – and why.
Step 3	When you're done, can you see any stakeholders with overlapping needs? Can a more supportive stakeholder help a more resistant stakeholder shift position? What's your plan to help more resistant stakeholders move to a more supportive stance?
	Write down any actions you need to take to manage your stakeholders in the box below.

Boundaries

Another word that's become important in modern life is boundaries. Many people don't have them or don't enforce them and end up doing things they don't really want to do. They're often known as 'People Pleasers' (a phrase that makes it sound like they're in the wrong). Many corporate people are People Pleasers. They're trained to be – through education and as they enter and succeed in the corporate world.

I quickly learnt, as do many people, that my success was directly linked to how good I made my bosses look. And in turn, how they made their bosses look.

The consequences can be burnout, as well as doing things that don't make you happy – or always proud of yourself.

Leaving all that behind presents an opportunity to install some boundaries so that you build the life you want.

Author Jessica Moore, wrote in her blog 'How to Manage Sensitivity with Healthy Boundaries' on Medium: 'Our boundaries define our personal space – and we need to be sovereign there in order to be able to step into our full power and potential.'

Stakeholder Mapping

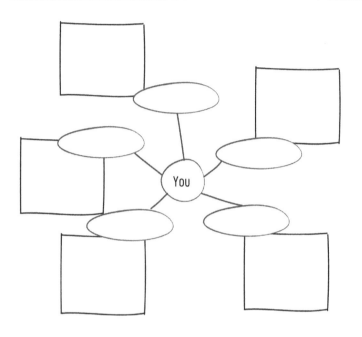

Stakeholder actions

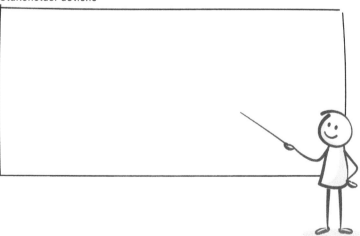

I love the idea of 'full power and potential'. It's what you probably expected to feel setting out on your corporate career, but quickly learnt was always just out of reach or in a few roles' time.

But now you've earnt the right to it! You may be looking for more flexibility, more purpose, more income, more autonomy, more creativity – as ingredients to unleash your power and potential.

These feed into your boundaries, your red lines. Places you need never feel obliged to cross again for the sake of managing your career or having no other option.

You get to decide.

Well, mostly.

Every freelancer, consultant, coach, in fact anyone who exchanges services for money, will find themselves in the awkward position of being pushed to do something they don't want to do.

I found myself being pushed to join a startup I didn't want to join. After numerous meetings with the founder, and hours of work on the startup's strategy, I realized I really didn't want to join him. I didn't want to build someone else's business – I wanted to build my own. This became a boundary I didn't realize I had until then, but it helped me reject other offers.

Similarly, I have some boundaries about the type of work I do – and the price I charge – even if I'm worried about cash flow. I have come to realize that I resent doing the wrong kind of work or not charging what I believe is a fair price – and that's no good for me or the client.

I have even turned down a project I really wanted to do, after a lot of consideration, because the client simply couldn't afford to pay me enough. These boundaries are important because otherwise there is a risk that you say 'yes' to everyone and ultimately dilute your offer and, consequently, your value. I believe it's a sure-fire way to unhappiness as well.

In our corporate jobs those boundaries exist – they're called things like strategy, approvals, budgets, department remits, roles, etc. Now you have to build your own.

Boundaries can be pretty easy to recognize because they tend to prompt an emotional response – anything from awkwardness to anxiety and even to rage.

You need to be especially brave here in defining what you want and what you don't want (especially the latter).

Values are a form of boundary. They have been done to death in corporates, leaving employees with often fairly bland, meaningless, undifferentiated words that are supposed to run deep throughout the whole workforce. But this is an opportunity to define values and behaviours that are highly distinctive and relevant for you. They can truly guide your decision-making, who you work with and the work you do. They provide a frame of reference for how you execute whatever you do next.

Boundaries in all their forms are core to your new position in the market and may need to be very consciously and intentionally repositioned when dealing with people you know from your corporate life. Or when they were your employer.

Rachel's story

I met Rachel (not her real name) a year or so after she left her corporate job as an account manager for an advertising agency. Part of the reason she had left was a toxic culture in her team, driven in large part by a boss who worked hard and played hard and expected everyone to do the same. Her boss made unreasonable demands of Rachel and others in the team, calling her during weekends and evenings asking for updates, slides and data without adequate time to prepare.

When Rachel left to set up her own niche marketing agency with a friend, her previous boss tried to subcontract Rachel's agency to execute some work for a client. Rachel was tempted because the money was good and she liked the client, but she declined the offer because working with that previous manager would conflict with her values – and that could impact Rachel's relationship with her business partner and the culture within their new business.

These boundaries can become hugely important in framing how you work and even what work you do. They may also limit the kinds of opportunities you will be able to take forward.

For instance, one of your boundaries might be putting family first, maybe after years where you felt they had come second. Being a consultant to the banking or legal profession may not be compatible with that boundary. Joining a soulful startup on a life-affirming mission may not be possible if one of your boundaries is earning an income in line with your corporate salary.

It's time to be honest with yourself (see Exercise 11).

Exercise 11: Boundary Conditions

Exercise instructions

Step 1	Jot down three or four boundaries that you feel instinctively will play a role in what you do next; red lines you will try not to cross (we're all human). Make them aspirational but not unrealistic or inauthentic.
Step 2	Next, try to describe why each one is important to you – what's driving it or creating the emotional response you're feeling.
Step 3	Then give each boundary a score out of five for how important it is under Strength of feeling – 1 for 'Bothersome' up to 5 for 'Seriously triggering'.
Step 4	Reflect on them a bit. What do you observe? Are they simple to avoid crossing? Are they compatible with the life you want to lead? Do any reinforce one another, or could they contradict? Is one more important than the others?

The rainbows and unicorns have been in short supply this chapter but it's important not to glamorize leaving behind your corporate job. There will be times when you find yourself on that veranda or wide awake at 3am, when you will be grateful for this preparation so you can step off or go back to sleep confident that you're ready and doing the right thing.

Boundary Conditions

Boundary				
Why it's important				
Strength of feeling				

Chapter summary

○ Preparation is key before you exit, to manage for a safe landing wherever you choose.

○ Walking away from a regular salary should not be undertaken without serious consideration and planning.

○ Corporate people can often place too much emphasis on the financial risk, quickly discounting the idea of leaving without properly working it through.

○ Corporates offer other financial and non-financial benefits which always need to be factored into the affordability of escaping the job.

o   Budgeting is a key strategy to understand the scale of the risk of leaving your job.

o   Building a buffer can help calm financial panic.

o   You have stakeholders in your decision to leave and they need managing in the same way as you would manage stakeholders in your job; you need to bring them along with you.

o   You have an opportunity to design the life you want by setting the right boundaries about the kind of work you want to do and how you want to do it.

CHAPTER 7

Why are you doing this?

'Find out who you are. And do it on purpose.'
Dolly Parton, Singer

As I said in the last chapter, cash isn't always the motivating force behind a move out of corporate life. Not because you can't potentially earn more money by setting up on your own, you can, but because there are often things that have become more important than money. Or because you've realized that more money won't make you any happier.

Struggling for purpose

I read so many books when I was in my corporate job, desperately trying to work out what my purpose was. I can't tell you how many times I did Simon Sinek's Golden Circles from 'Find your why'. I didn't feel any connection to anything with any depth beyond being here for my family, providing for them financially, morally, educationally, etc.

Purpose asks probably the biggest question any human will ask: Why am I here?

It's too big for many of us. Especially when we're also trying to get the kids off to school, dress ourselves and deal with a barrage of notifications on our phones.

I'm also not sure I trust myself to get my purpose right. Or even for there to be just one purpose.

And if I'm really honest, I'm not sure I really need work to be so connected with something as deep as purpose. I work to live not the other way round.

But my absence of purpose actually made me feel a bit empty when it came to my job. Was it, shock horror, just a means to an end?

I even remember faking it in a training session once, just to say something. Showing a link between my job and the company's purpose. Telling myself and others why I got out of bed each morning. What rubbish.

Today, I get myself out of bed each morning because I want to get on with my day – and even when I don't. I'm not sure much has really changed.

I still feel hugely motivated to earn enough money to build a happy life for my family, one that gives us all the best chance of being healthy and successful.

Maybe that's enough of a purpose. For me at least.

This book is a practical guide. If you've nailed your purpose, I'm glad for you. It's harder for many of us. And if you feel it's adding a degree of pressure to 'find your purpose', don't worry – I don't believe it's essential for a happy and fulfilled life on planet earth.

But I do think you need to be clear on what you're expecting from your move out of corporate life.

This chapter will help you get clear.

You've uncovered all those amazing things you can do, you've been honest with yourself about some of the constraints you face, and which ones can be overcome and which ones can't. Now you need to look forward.

What are you doing this for?

Because quite honestly, it's probably easier to stay put. You can, you know. It's perfectly acceptable. In fact, it's more socially acceptable than what you're thinking of doing. It's more 'normal'.

If that's what you want.

I suspect it isn't or you wouldn't have got to Chapter 7.

So let's get clear on what you do want and, specifically, what you want work to be like.

Work is good for us. It challenges us, it occupies us, it develops us, it connects us with others. Most people reading this book aren't looking to leave corporate life to do nothing, so work it is.

Asking yourself 'What do you want work to be like?' gives you greater freedom of choice over what you do next than finding your life's purpose. It's much more about how you work, how you get your energy, how you feel fulfilled. 'How' is more expansive than 'What', but more pragmatic and realistic than 'Why'. IMHO.

Despite my glass half full assertion earlier, I actually find this question works best for people if you ask the opposite: What don't you want work to be like?

Now it's time for Exercise 12.

Exercise 12: Drains And Energizers

Exercise instructions

Step 1	Think about times at work when you've felt really frustrated, squashed or unhappy, maybe a period when you've gone home wanting to jack it all in. Why was that? Which of your needs were challenged? Had work become a drudge? Were you feeling undervalued? Was there a disabling culture in place? A weak leader?
Step 2	Part one of this exercise is to write down what drained you in the left-hand side of the model.
	You may begin.

Drains And Energizers

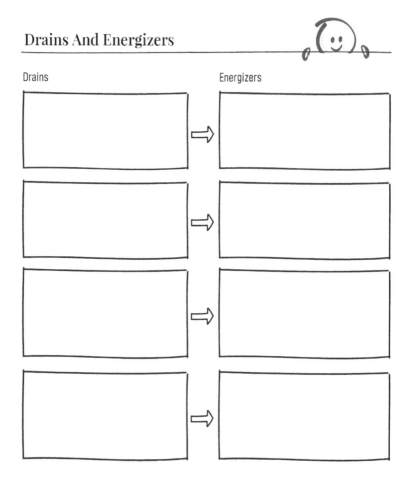

Drains

Energizers

Through this exercise I realized my top three Drains at work were:

1 Routine: I hate to do the same thing more than once, I don't like running processes or feeling like a cog. I actually don't like it when there are no surprises in my day.

2 Micro-management: I hate having someone looking over my shoulder, marking my work, telling me how to do something or when to do it.

3 Over-working: I hate going slow, being held up or working with procrastinators or perfectionists. I hate meetings where people just talk and stop me getting on.

I don't sound that easy to work with I know, quite awful to manage in fact. I look back now and think how did I survive for so long in corporate jobs characterized by routines, rules, hierarchies and deathly pace? I suspect I was unhappy for much longer than I admitted. I suspect for much of the time I was faking it.

Part two of the exercise is to flip the Drains into Energizers. To give you a guide mine looks like the following diagram.

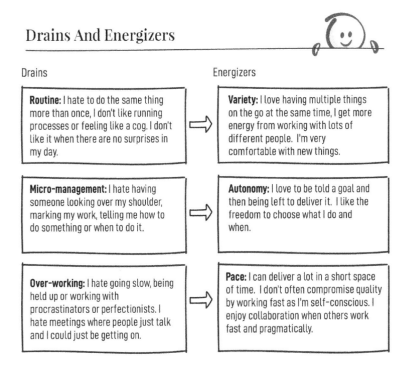

Drains And Energizers

Drains	Energizers
Routine: I hate to do the same thing more than once, I don't like running processes or feeling like a cog. I don't like it when there are no surprises in my day.	**Variety:** I love having multiple things on the go at the same time, I get more energy from working with lots of different people. I'm very comfortable with new things.
Micro-management: I hate having someone looking over my shoulder, marking my work, telling me how to do something or when to do it.	**Autonomy:** I love to be told a goal and then being left to deliver it. I like the freedom to choose what I do and when.
Over-working: I hate going slow, being held up or working with procrastinators or perfectionists. I hate meetings where people just talk and I could just be getting on.	**Pace:** I can deliver a lot in a short space of time. I don't often compromise quality by working fast as I'm self-conscious. I enjoy collaboration when others work fast and pragmatically.

I think I sound a lot nicer now. But I don't sound like a corporate team player. I see that now in a way I didn't before.

Give it a go for your Energizers.

Step 3	Flip your Drains into Energizers – find an opposite to each one and write something that fills you with energy and plays to your strengths.

Knowing *how I want* to work has given me a filter for the kind of work I do best – and has informed some of my boundaries (see Chapter 6):

o   I have turned down work with people when I didn't think they would work at my pace.

o   I have turned down work with people who wanted to slow me down with a process I didn't believe in.

o   I have turned down work that's been more-of-the-same and lacked the variety I need for energy.

o   I have counter-offered different ways of working to secure work that aligned better with how I best work.

I lacked this self-knowledge before and didn't always understand why I was unhappy and frustrated. It's helped me better understand what I need from work.

Your North Star

When you're tested or distracted, your North Star acts as a beacon, a guiding light. It's a simple concept that works well for organizations to marshal teams and individuals around a single priority.

Sean Ellis, author of *Hacking Growth*, coined the phrase 'North Star Metric' to help organizations, particularly startups paralyzed by too many objectives, to focus on the most important one.

For some organizations it's revenue, for others it's new customers, for others it might be clickthrough rate. For an e-commerce retailer it might be basket size, for a subscription business it might be monthly recurring revenue.

You might be thinking what has this got to do with me?

The North Star drives singularity of mission – if everyone in the organization is behind an app's monthly average users, then anything that does not contribute to that metric does not get prioritized.

I think it's a good way to think about any major change and what you want from it. Only when you have this singularity of focus will you know you have succeeded or that where you have landed feels right.

And 'feels right' might be more useful to you than a hard metric like income.

For me the North Star is a blend between my three needs from work: Variety, Autonomy and Pace. When all three needs are aligned I reckon I'm in flow. When I'm doing too much of one thing for too long (like writing a book), I get anxious and become much less efficient. When someone at home or at work limits my autonomy or slows me down in some way, my hackles rise and I waste time being uncooperative and moaning to myself.

I don't need a hard metric for this because it's just me. I recognize the feeling when I'm in alignment with my North Star and that's sufficient.

But you might want something harder, more measurable. Maybe you want to stop work entirely by the time you're 60, or even 50. Maybe you want to create enough 'passive income' (where you earn money in your sleep) to fund your life. Maybe you want to work three days a week or four hours. Maybe you want to build a legacy.

In a way this goes back to the Forces of Change model in Chapter 4 – what does progress look like for you? Project forward and ask yourself 'What would my most successful me look like?'

Your Return on Disruption

While the North Star gives you a useful frame to decide how you work and whether the life you're leading is aligned, you need goals to get things done. It's a bit like business thinker Peter Drucker's distinction between leadership and management in The Effective Executive: '"Management is doing things right; leadership is doing the right things."'.

Your North Star ensures you're working on the 'right things'. Goals make sure you do 'things right' and give you focus. They're measurable so you know whether you are where you expect to be.

When you leave your job, a gaping hole can emerge, called the 'rest of your life' which is both terrifying and incredibly easy to fritter away: 'Crikey where has the week/month/year gone?'

You need to use all your corporate superpowers to get focused on what you want to get out of this move. What is your expected Return on Disruption, or RoD?

It's easier to stay put. There will be moments during the transition and for several years after where your life will feel harder than it did in your corporate career – especially as absence makes the heart grow fonder and you may not remember why the bad old days were so bad.

Sharp, focused goals will set your expectations and will provide a benchmark against which you can measure your performance and success or failure.

I don't need to explain how to define goals to a corporate person. You've had SMART rammed down your neck for decades. But do you know about OKRs? Objectives and Key Results? They're a tool that author of *Measure what Matters*, John Doerr, introduced at Intel, then at Google, and the tech community has jumped on them, in line with the agile bandwagon, to provide focus to software delivery. Many organizations, including corporates, use OKRs today. Even Bono from the band U2 is a fan, joining John on stage to talk about how OKRs can create the framework to turn passions into actions into outcomes.

And, given you're shaking things up, why not take a stab at using them to get clear what you want from your move, what's your expected RoD?

They're far from rocket science: Objective is your high-level goal and the Key Results are what you can measure, i.e. the SMART bit.

So you might have something simple like this:

o   Objective: Work more flexibly around my family.

o   Key result: Work no more than four days a week.

o   Key result: Take a break 4pm–6pm to do the school run and check in with the kids over dinner.

Or

o Objective: Replace the income I had from my former corporate job.

o Key result: Within one year I will earn £X a month.

You can imagine in the corporate world you would need a full day workshop to come up with something like this, to which everyone agreed and signed off.

And there would be a high risk of compromise and sand-bagging taking the edge off some of those Key Results. Now you're liberated from all that, it's just about you (and those you care about)… what's your Objective from this move and how will you know if you're successful?

John advocates weekly check-ins on your OKRs. For some OKRs, like 'building flexibility around family', weekly might be the right cadence. For others, like the income one, it's too frequent. But learn from your corporate days – don't make the goals something you do at the beginning of the year and only look at just before the end.

OK?

Now it's time for Exercise 13.

Exercise 13: OKRs

Exercise instructions

Write down your top three or four OKRs for your corporate exit.

Step 1	For now give yourself a timeframe of a year – that's far enough to feel like you'll be in a different place from now, but close enough that you can visualize moving to that place. Start with your Objective – something quite broad and reasonably ambitious.
Step 2	Then add one to three Key Results, by which you will be able to judge that the Objective has been met. Something that every few weeks you could consult to see if you're making progress – and, if not, plan the necessary interventions.

Step 3   Now ask yourself 'How do these OKRs fit with the energizers you identified in in Chapter 5 and your North Star?'

Remember, this book is a place for your notes. You don't need to feel hamstrung or locked to what you write here. You can always go to corporateescapology.com/tools to download the exercise template to write down as many versions of your OKRs until you're happy.

OKRs

Objective	Key results

Bringing everything together

Part II of this book has been about getting to know yourself better – where you're strong and your energy lies, and why you're doing this and what you're looking to achieve.

I want you to pull all this great thinking into your Escape Plan Canvas now (see the Appendix). I'm a big fan of one page canvases where you can write out everything that matters, identify gaps and test out any inconsistencies. I also like how they can act as powerful communication tools to explain your thinking to yourself and to others.

You've got a lot to update here – in those two middle columns: the constraints you face (financial and non-financial), the primary stakeholders you need to manage, your boundaries and red lines – and now your SEKSE list and your OKRs.

You can download the canvas from corporateescapology.com/ tools or scribble here.

I would really recommend printing out the exercise template and writing things out a few times until you're happy enough to share it with others. And then stick it up on your wall. You will need it, particularly in your first year, to remind yourself why you're doing this – and that you **can** do this!

Chapter summary

o   Explore why you want to make the leap out of your corporate career to properly understand your motivations; write them down.

o   Without clarity and, ideally, singularity in motivation, there's a risk of making bad choices that will not lead to the outcomes you're seeking.

o   How you want to work may be more important to you than the type of work you want to do.

o   Don't get hung up on purpose and why you are here if it doesn't help you move forward.

○ Setting goals will provide more focus and specificity to the outcomes you expect from your move; OKRs (Objectives and Key Results) can help.

○ Precision is less important in setting mission and goals at this stage because there are many unknowns – but it's always easier to evolve your thinking from something written down than trusting your brain to keep track.

III Explore your options

In Part I, I talked about how much the world of work has changed over last few decades, and particularly since the pandemic. A multiplicity of factors, including technology, globalization, urbanization, improved health and living standards has fundamentally, and irrevocably, changed how we work today and what we expect from work.

Part III of the Escape Method is about opening your eyes to that world.

It will do two things:

1   Inspire you to see how others are using their skills, experience and know-how to make this New World work for them.

2   Build your self-confidence – if these people can do it, why
can't you?

You'll meet characters who spent years, even decades, building
corporate careers and now use everything they've learnt to
lead lives that serve them better.

Under each story I've added some practical inspiration, ideas
and resources you can take away to explore further.

It's time to open your mind!

CHAPTER 8

New pathways

'You have brains in your head. You have feet in your shoes. You can steer yourself any direction you choose... Oh, the Places You Will Go!'

Dr Seuss, Author

I want this chapter to be a smorgasbord of delectable stories from other Corporate Escapologists that inspire you. But don't worry, it's not the career equivalent of showing you travel brochures for Mauritius when you're broke or have used up all your holiday.

Instead, it will help you think more broadly and creatively about what work could be for you – with examples from people who are living those lives now.

They are living those lives now BECAUSE of the investment of time and energy in building their careers in corporate organizations. They haven't been lucky or winged it.

They have worked for it.

And you have too.

Experimentation

But before jumping in, I want to say a word about experimentation. It's become pretty trendy in meetings to say, 'let's run an experiment'. And like many of the trendy things in corporate life, it originated in startup life, as the good startups quickly realized that trying things in the real world is usually better than imagining how things will work in the real world – from inside a meeting room.

Corporates don't really like experiments, even if they say they do. Experiments are risky. You can't plan them in detail. You can't know the outcome. They don't comply with the mountain of process. And they might result in a knock to reputation if things don't work out.

But experimentation is part of your post-corporate transition. And it's a huge part of de-risking your move, so that you leap successfully and never come to regret what you've done.

When I left BP, I very consciously decided that my first year was going to be my year of experimentation. Trying lots of different things to see what felt right.

For more than 20 years I'd never done anything other than take orders from someone a level or two above me and execute those orders. Every day.

I wasn't completely convinced I could trust myself to pick the right options straight away, and I didn't want to regret closing other options off too early.

I knew I wanted to scratch my entrepreneurial itch, I wanted to write, I didn't want to lose my technical content, I fancied myself as a bit of an expert, I wanted to mentor startups.

So I did them all.

> I was incredibly lucky to get some consultancy lined up before I'd left my job. A former colleague had posted a nice message about me on LinkedIn. A CEO of a medium-sized company in his network saw that message, asked me for a chat and years later I'm still doing some really fun marketing consultancy with his firm.

A friend from McKinsey asked me to talk about how I'd built culture within my corporate career to his clients – I'm still asked to do this several years later, giving me a lovely badge of honour on my CV and LinkedIn profile.

I wrote a weekly blog called Corporate Escapologist.

I mentored for three startup accelerators: Techstars, Carbon 13 and then with Startupbootcamp – which turned into a paid job a few years later.

I learnt a lot from these experiments, some of which could be described as successful. But there were others that were less successful, where I learnt more about myself and what I really wanted.

I joined a couple of startups, before realizing they weren't for me (they lacked the variety and autonomy I was seeking).

I built a product business, turning my know-how about customer discovery into a tool for startups (it failed because, somewhat ironically, I targeted the wrong customer).

I set up a learning platform to teach people how to understand their customer better.

I enrolled in some courses to see if I wanted to retrain or go back to university (always tempting, thankfully too expensive).

I bought a dozen website addresses for schemes that went nowhere (wasting only a few pounds at a time).

This is a moment you may not get many times in your life to try lots of things, even if they seem unrelated, impractical or unlikely to succeed. Use this opportunity wisely, don't imagine you know everything about yourself. Instead, try to learn in the real world, not just in your head, where you're prone to discount something before you've given it a shot.

And fail. Because the risk is low. You may not even need to fail fast. It took almost two years for my product business to fail before I finally accepted it. If I'd failed faster, I might never have got the job with Startupbootcamp. I might even have accepted a corporate job offer.

Trying also doesn't necessarily mean you need to go 'all in'. You can dip your toe into something – or observe from the side-lines. Shadow someone or talk to someone doing what you want to do. Experiment vicariously!

But I really do sincerely recommend you try everything you have a hunch you might enjoy.

Other people's stories

Over the past few years I have collected other people's stories about how they left corporate life and what they did next. This has inspired me and helped validate the Escape Method (Detach, Audit, Explore, Exit and Sustain). I've seen how these people have lived the model without realizing that they were all following a pattern. And you can too.

Prepare to be inspired.

Katie, the author

Katie trained as a journalist but over time became more fascinated by how the content that she and other journalists produced was distributed to the customer. She first moved into a website role, and eventually into product, where she pulled together a cross-functional team to build products for customers.

Katie worked for ten years at ICIS, a news, data and analytics provider, before deciding to up-sticks and go traveling for a year, with her partner, a nine year old and a three year old!

Katie had an idea of building an advisory business for others considering family travel and wrote an account of her travels along the way. She even got some PR about her plans, getting on to the front cover of the Sunday Times Money Supplement and she was off. It sounds like they had the adventure of a lifetime, trials, tribulations and tonnes of memorable experiences. But when Katie returned, her plan of helping others follow her example faded fast.

Travel had been severely restricted in 2020–2022 due to the COVID-19 pandemic. So her business idea was put to one side. Instead, Katie looked to the skills, experiences and know-how she'd acquired during her corporate career and began to use her product skills as a consultant with small businesses and local government.

She eventually decided to write a book about better understanding customers – especially geared to small business owners, an unserved niche she'd validated on Instagram. She built a following, got a book deal, wrote the book and now it's published – it's called 'Do Penguins Eat Peaches?' and it's terrific.

You can find Katie on LinkedIn (search: Katie Tucker), Instagram (@productjungle) or visit her at productjungle. co.uk where you can also buy her book.

You can hear more of Katie's story on the Corporate Escapology podcast.

Practical inspiration

One thing both Katie and I have learnt is that the book is just a part of your marketing strategy – it gives you authority, a distinctive position and it forces you to develop and articulate your offer. It is not a business by itself. But it supports your coaching, consulting, education, professional speaker... fill in the gap... business.

If you're thinking about writing a book, I would highly recommend Practical Inspiration Publishing's 10 day Business Book Proposal Challenge which both Katie and I have done. Ten gruelling days to write a competent book proposal and get feedback, including publisher contacts – as well as a chance for one aspiring author to win a book deal. I didn't win by the way – but I went on to Alison's This Book Means Business Bootcamp, which is the only way I managed to finish this one.

Niall, the startup founder

I met Niall scouting for startups for the accelerator programme I run for Startupbootcamp. He runs an electric vehicle charging business called Paua, but although he has serial entrepreneurial tendencies, he spent 20 years in very traditional corporates, EDF and SSE.

He was a consummate side-hustler: once he imported a tonne of jackfruit and hawked it around healthfood retailers, including Wholefoods. Another time he built a solar business that collapsed overnight when the UK government closed its subsidy-based FEED tariff scheme. A further time he worked pro bono (free of charge) to start up a local energy community. His first business was as a professional photographer at age 18; he started young.

Niall is one of those guys who keeps a book of startup ideas. Even now.

When I met him, I thought 'this guy knows himself really well'. He was open about his flaws and failures – 'I'm a people pleaser', 'I can let people down by saying yes too often', 'I did a bad job there'. But he is also very clued into his strengths. While at EDF, he took lots of leadership courses, tonnes of psychometric tests and read voraciously. And he used what he learnt about himself to test his thinking with other successful people. He would book time with execs in his company to ask them how they succeeded – so he could learn for himself.

The result is Niall is a very different type of entrepreneur. He's robust, resilient and a safe pair of hands. He's smart, because he's learnt a lot in just a few key areas – and, even then, as he told me, 'I only need to know a bit more than everyone else'.

His repeated attempts to build startups inside corporates, alongside the security of a monthly salary, meant he learnt a lot without taking much risk. One lesson that he implemented for his latest startup, Paua, was he wanted a co-founder – he didn't want to build a business on his own again.

Niall's chance of success is higher than many founders because of his corporate experience. That's not something you can say about many entrepreneurs – in many ways the cultures clash

– but in Niall's case his entrepreneurial instincts have stronger foundations than many entrepreneurs, because of his experience in corporate life. He invested time in learning how to business-build inside the safety of his corporate environment – and play to his strengths to become a great entrepreneur.

You can find Niall on LinkedIn (search: Niall Riddell) or visit his startup Paua at pauatech.com.

You can hear more of Niall's story on the Corporate Escapology podcast.

Practical inspiration

It's never been easier to start up your own business and reinvent yourself as a founder. But just because something is easier doesn't make it more likely to succeed.

There are some great, and rather obvious, books to read: Lean Startup, Four Steps to the Epiphany, Zero to One, Business Model Generation (see the Further reading section at the end of the book).

Having been there, I think now I would follow Niall's lesson of finding a co-founder and not do it again on my own. But the main thing I've taken away is Niall's focus on building something that hits squarely in the middle of a three-way Venn diagram: 1) I see a big customer problem, 2) I care about solving it and 3) I believe I have the skills and experience to solve it.

Another thing I see in Niall, that often corporate people lack, is a willingness to start doing something, sometimes anything – and get customer feedback. 'Do' rather than 'Think' and test with real people, not inside your head.

I learnt late the difference between customers who are mildly interested and ones that are in urgent need of what you're offering. Spend time only with the latter.

There's another book in me for this one, but in the meantime you can find plenty of blogs I've written on these topics and what I was learning (mainly by screwing up) at corporateescapologist. substack.com when I was building my own product startup.

Chris, the startup founder

Chris took a different approach to transitioning to startup life – with more structure, skills-building and support.

Chris worked in venture capital for six years, but he'd got itchy feet and signed up to a three-month coding bootcamp in Barcelona. Here he learnt more than just coding, but also how to build prototypes and more about the data landscape. He left VC to start his own AI-based climate-technology business, PropEco, and to do some good.

Chris applied to join a number of startup accelerator programmes to speed up his development as a founder. First, he joined Carbon 13, a climate accelerator based in Cambridge UK, and more recently he joined a geo-spatial, domain-specific accelerator called Geovation, run by the UK Ordnance Survey, in association with the UK Land Registry.

Through Geovation, Chris gained some funding, as well as met domain experts, mentors and business leaders, and attended workshops and classes to learn how to successfully build his business. Moreover, being part of a recognized programme, Chris unlocked further opportunities for both funding and technology trials.

You can find Chris on LinkedIn (search: Chris Hardman) or visit his startup PropEco at propeco.io.

Practical inspiration

With hundreds of startup accelerators around the world, there is considerable choice for a startup looking to gain access to proven methodologies, mentors and experts, and in some cases funding – often in exchange for equity. There are other ecosystem players like venture-builders and startup studios where you can pay for programmes and mentoring of the type provided by accelerators, with or without needing to give up equity in your business.

Here are a few:

o   Startupbootcamp (who I mentor for), Techstars, Plug and Play: more traditional accelerators where existing startups apply to join programmes and trade equity for funding, skills-building, mentoring and access to networks.

o Entrepreneur First, Antler, Zinc, Carbon 13 where individuals are selected and matched to other co-founders and together identify and build an equity-funded business.

Many websites run annual lists of the best startup accelerator programmes and how each provides differentiated value.

Steve, the serial board member and potter

Steve worked at BP for almost 25 years, mostly in innovation and technology commercialization. He is fundamentally a strategist with a superpower in connecting disparate things, risks and opportunities, to create new value. He is unusually both very big picture and fastidious. He makes beautiful Japanese/Scandinavian-inspired pots and turns wood to make beautiful household objects from lighting to tables.

During his last five years at BP he set up a venture-builder to take a mixture of home-grown and acquired technologies and commercialize them as startups which could potentially be spun-out and scaled as standalone businesses. During this time he was invited to sit on a number of boards and eventually chair some.

When he left BP, he decided to take his board advisory skills and turn them into a substantive source of income. This has left him time, often as much as a third of a week, to turn his passion for ceramics into a small business.

Steve can add tremendous value to the boards on which he sits for relatively short bursts of time; it's mostly structured around a planned quarterly cadence, so he can fit other things he loves around the work he knows he's good at. Like being an advisor to a purpose-led fund and to several high-tech startups – as well as making beautiful ceramics and showcasing them in several high-end galleries around the UK.

You can find Steve on LinkedIn (search: Stephen Cook) or visit his beautiful ceramics business on Instagram at instagram.com/stevecook__ and at authorinteriors.com/meet-the-makers/steve-cook.

You can hear more of Steve's story on the Corporate Escapology podcast.

Practical inspiration

Steve made a smart move getting experience when he was still with BP rather than trying to find board positions afterwards with only corporate experience. Most employers will allow employees to sit on boards as non-executive directors (NEDs) – although this should be declared to avoid any potential conflicts of interest.

I met Louise Broekman, chief executive of the Advisory Board Centre (advisoryboardcentre.com), as part of my research for this book. Louise runs a global network of experienced professionals and is on a mission to raise standards of the global advisory sector, through training, accreditation and research. It might be a good place to start if you want to develop board-level or advisory board skills and understand the associated obligations.

Agencies, like VirtualNonExecs and Nurole, also exist to source high-quality NEDs and board members.

Before leaving, talk to these groups to explore whether your skillset would be valuable and in-demand – or whether you would benefit from more experience or training.

Tom, the digital marketing freelancer

I met Tom Coleman on Instagram and we did a 'Live' together where he shared his journey just as he was transitioning from corporate employee in Marketing and Communications to working for himself as a freelancer.

It's a classic move out of a corporate job, using the skills developed for one client (your employer) and offering them to multiple clients. It's not without risk however, but Tom did a few clever things to de-risk the leap.

Firstly, he built a solid following on Instagram of over 7,000 people before he left. By regularly posting, adding value, and opening up about his journey, he built great connections with his followers, some of whom were the first buyers when he announced he was going freelance.

Secondly, he didn't cut the cord with his corporate and leave immediately. Through open and honest conversations with his employer he agreed a staged exit plan, working part-time and gradually phasing out, reducing the risk of zero income during his transition to freelance.

Now he has cut the cord and filled his pipeline with lovely clients he's met almost exclusively on Instagram, offering social media management, one-to-one coaching, workshops and a marketing membership called 'The Growth Club'.

Follow Tom on Instagram @imtomcoleman or visit imtomcoleman.com

Practical inspiration

This leap can be de-risked by scouting for potential clients before you leave. It requires clarity around your offer, so potential customers know what they're getting – so they can decide whether it's what they want. Watch out for any contractual clauses that stop you working with previous competitors or clients for periods after you leave.

Some people have success with online freelancer marketplaces (links below). I have worked with clients who have successfully found long-term freelancers here; it's not all low-paid gigs.

Networks are very important – LinkedIn is critical as well as real-life events. The key is being able to crisply explain what you do and how you can help.

Online freelancer marketplaces: Upwork.com, Fiverr.com, Peopleperhour.com

Charlie, the online course creator

I met Charlie through Instagram. She was one of the first people I tested some of the Corporate Escapology tools and templates on as she wondered 'What if?' when thinking about an alternative career path.

Charlie worked for Accenture for almost five years and before that Sky, and was working as head of service operations for a large retail group. But alongside these corporate roles, Charlie had been running a digital marketing services agency for more than seven years, targeting the luxury hotel sector. When I met her, Charlie was clear about the conditions necessary to move full-time to the marketing agency – she needed several more clients on retainer. This was a struggle while she worked full-time.

We went back to basics, to look more deeply at both what she wanted from a move and also where her skills, experiences and know-how lay. This opened up discussions about another side-hustle Charlie had begun after Accenture: setting up a YouTube channel to help new entrants into the consulting industry learn fast from an insider. Whilst at Accenture, Charlie had mentored, and even run training sessions, for new consultants, because she'd found them lacking the basic skills to be useful when she was a consultant team leader.

During our sessions it became clear that Charlie was still passionate about this mission and had a unique skillset (consultant/digital marketing/service operations) to be able to commercialize the business. She set up Consulting Survival as a content business, relying on subscriptions and coaching. She now offers distinctive, domain-specific content through YouTube and a weekly newsletter, pulling together industry needs to help consultants keep one step ahead of their clients.

Alongside this, Charlie works as a consultant to provide an income as Consulting Survival builds.

Follow Charlie on YouTube @consultingcharlie6044 or visit consultingsurvival.com.

You can hear more of Charlie's story on the Corporate Escapology podcast.

Practical inspiration
Charlie's experience bears out the advice many startup founders hear: find what drives you, find what you're uniquely good at and find what your customers want. She had tested the latter, building a niche following on YouTube that validated her hypotheses and now she already has a customer base to target her new content and platform.

Charlie's experiments are effectively free to run through social media and a web platform, but she could invest in some Google or Facebook adverts to drive more traffic and run tests with larger groups. By capping her daily spend, Charlie could still make these experiments low-cost but test one approach versus another (A/B test), test demand with a landing page before she's invested in building a product or even tested user engagement with a fake automated product, managed manually in the background (called a Wizard of Oz).

The Strategyzer series (strategyzer.com), developed by Alexander Osterwalder and David Bland, has lots of great tools to help early-stage businesses find their customers and de-risk their businesses. My favourite is their book, *Testing Business Ideas: A Field Guide for Rapid Experimentation*, which has tonnes of ideas to test for desirability, feasibility and viability.

 Erica the coach

Erica read my blog and said it felt like I was in her head so we spoke and hit it off straightaway. She'd worked at BP, though our paths had never crossed. She was a tough offshore operations leader while I was a head office-type far from the front line.

An engineer, having worked in offshore Angola, the Alaskan North Slope, in Azerbaijan and Georgia delivering one of the world's biggest transnational gas pipelines, Erica's career moved into technology and even mergers and acquisitions. She always worked in high-pressured environments, where cultures and people are really tested – and don't always come off well.

Erica left BP to pursue her passion of helping organizations and individuals build more Diverse, Equitable and Inclusive (DEI) workplaces.

She set up Two Piers as a Public Benefit Organization, offering coaching, consultancy and workshops.

As a woman working in an extremely isolated, high-hazard and very male-dominated environment, Erica has lots to share. Some of her stories left my jaw wide open. And they formed the starting point for her coaching and consulting business.

She spent several years getting qualified as a coach, building her coaching style, practising on people like me before going hard on the DEI angle – positioning herself as an expert, someone who has been there and someone who can help.

Erica's coaching carries gravitas because she's worked in such extreme settings. She can empathize very easily with how her clients feel and, through her own lived experience, can help them work through their challenges.

She also offers workshops and runs consultancy projects for teams trying to bring about change within their own organizations.

Follow Erica on LinkedIn (search: Erica D'Eramo) or visit twopiersconsulting.com.

You can hear more of Erica's story on the Corporate Escapology podcast.

Practical inspiration
Coaching covers a broad spectrum from executive and business coaching to group coaching or programme-based coaching.

I offer a type of career-coaching that helps people who have decided to leave their corporate jobs prepare and transition.

Coaching can bleed into mentoring too, which typically offers more domain expertise and is potentially more directive.

There are qualifications and affiliated bodies in which you might want to invest. Learning to coach and finding your own style of coaching is critical to your success and training can undoubtedly help here.

Coaching organizations:

o International Coaching Federation – coachingfederation. org

o Association for Coaching – associationforcoaching.com

o European Mentoring and Coaching Council – emccglobal. org

David the consultant

David worked for 17 years in a corporate IT department, specializing in data management. Throughout his time at the company he accumulated considerable experience, qualifications and network. He spoke at conferences, wrote technical papers and contributed to several books. He was recognized as an expert within his technical community.

He was made redundant as part of a merger and jumped at the opportunity to exit corporate life and take a year off before deciding what to do next. But within weeks his phone was ringing with people in his network asking if he could help them with a problem. He hadn't planned on becoming a consultant, but the opportunity presented itself and, with some advice from a friend on setting up a limited company, pricing and building a website, he set himself up as a one-man band.

With the benefit of technologies like Zoom and Calendly, David was able to carve out three half days a week when he made himself available for single-hour slots. Each slot was paid with a credit card, making expenses easy for his clients – and ensuring he didn't work more hours than planned.

Within six months of his network being aware of his availability, David had most of his slots booked for most weeks and was making the same income as his previous job!

Practical inspiration
David's experience shows what is possible with a technical skillset in demand – and a network that wants to access it. This may be neither feasible nor desirable for everyone, but there are routes to market like this for a consultant – right up to project work, based on a day rate or on an overall project cost.

Consultants thrive on networks. David was fortunate having built an external one over many years, which he could access afterwards. Prioritizing network-building before leaving the corporate is vital in order to de-risk the leap.

There are many flexible, on-demand marketplaces these days to connect consultants to businesses looking for skilled consultants (see the following list). Local business network organizations, like the Chambers of Commerce, can be good places to explore local consulting opportunities, along with events and conferences. In addition, there are meetups covering all manner of interest-groups these days, which can be in-person or online.

o   Meetup: meetup.com

o   Event Brite: eventbrite.com

o   Entrepreneurs Circle: entrepreneurscircle.org

o   Flexible on-demand consulting marketplaces: Freshminds. co.uk, Movemeon.com, Catalant.com, Expert360.com

Claire, community architect

Claire qualified as a lawyer and spent ten years working as a solicitor. It was never her dream job, but she'd been persuaded by its stability and status and found success. However, she always had a sense that there could be more.

One day she stumbled on a YouTube video about new digital marketing services – search engine optimization, online ads, social media, etc. Claire was taken by the idea and went on a weekend course to learn more. During that weekend she learnt

lots of different online marketing skills, but one stood out: community marketing.

Claire liked the sound of building communities of people who cared about something and who wanted to spend time with other people who felt the same. She decided to leave the law and set up by herself, helping businesses access the power of community marketing, alongside other consultancy, building teams and culture. She became a Community Architect.

During this time she attended the DO Lectures, run by David Hieatt, to help sharpen her offer. She met lots of people just like her, small business owners, entrepreneurs, makers, consultants and coaches, and she noticed common problems of isolation and a lack of support.

Claire talked to David after his course and asked if he'd support her inviting people from her group to join a new community. He agreed and after running an informal community over Zoom for a few months, Claire formed Like Hearted Leaders, an online business network with a mission to end loneliness in leadership.

Each Friday, Claire brings the community together at 8.30–9.30am, where members share what's been going on in their lives and where they're struggling or succeeding. Claire breaks them into smaller groups to discuss a particular issue or question and then the group shares back where the discussion leads. The topics can be challenging and really thought-provoking. I know because I was a member.

Most corporate people would say it feels like a really supportive team meeting. Claire brings in guest speakers (many are members) and also holds extra sessions through the week, for example, 'Creative Breakfasts' where everyone joins a call to write for 20 minutes.

Members pay a monthly subscription to join Like Hearted Leaders and the group has even published its own book, On a Friday. Members can promote their services to one another, with swapping and bartering commonplace where one member has skills another lacks. But it is community that Claire is really providing to her members, a place where people find like-minded, supportive people who want to help.

It may be a far cry from her days as a solicitor, but her experience has not been lost. Anyone who has worked with Claire appreciates the care, attention to detail and quality in everything she does – it's part of how she unconsciously leads and shares her expertise.

Like Hearted Leaders gives Claire purpose and fulfilment, but it also provides her with a case study in how community can be an effective marketing tool to reach and nurture clients and generate revenue.

Follow Claire on LinkedIn (search: Claire Perry-Louise) or visit likeheartedleaders.com.

You can hear more of Claire's story on the Corporate Escapology podcast.

 Practical inspiration

By attending a weekend course on something radically different from her day job, Claire opened herself up to different career options to see what interested her most. Community marketing stood out and she not only learnt more about it but had experts on hand to probe deeper.

The DO lectures gave Claire a strong insight into her customers and their specific pain points around loneliness and a lack of support. She built her community over time, not rushing to build volume and thereby compromising what made it special and appealing to her members.

Having built her own successful community, Claire now has the credibility to help others build theirs, as well as offer ancillary services in marketing and culture.

 Martin, investing in an asset

Many of us dream of escaping the rat race, moving to the country and buying a country pile with a holiday letting business.

Martin is one of those people who didn't just dream it, he is doing it.

He spent 32 (!) years working for Johnson Matthey in a variety of commercial and technical roles, ran numerous business units and was most recently JM's Group Strategy Director. In 2019 Martin left to pursue his dream.

However, his exit coincided with the onset of the COVID-19 pandemic which hit hospitality hard. So Martin pressed pause on his dream and went back to reality. His reality, where he could use his corporate – and particularly his battery technology – skills, experience and know-how to help others. He took on a number of Non-Executive Director roles for several cleantech startups, as well as Chair of the Audit Committee of ITM Power plc, a hydrogen technology scale-up.

During 2023, Martin and his partner left London and found a holiday letting business for sale in Cumbria, just outside the beautiful Lake District. They bought it, renovated it and opened for business in spring 2024.

Unlike many corporate careerists these days, which tend towards functional specialisms, Martin ran entire businesses for Johnson Matthey. He was accountable for their profit and loss, developing and executing strategy, including mergers and acquisitions. He knows what it takes to build a business and make it profitable.

Only now, it's going to be for his family.

Practical inspiration
Investing in an asset, even property, may be a higher risk than setting up to sell services, like consultancy, but it affords an opportunity to build a lifestyle business, as well as build an investment for the future, a legacy. If all goes well, Martin and his partner will have built a more valuable asset with a regular return on investment long into their deferred retirement.

Martin wanted a country house with land, but his commercial instincts told him it had to pay for itself. This way, he gets the house and land funded by rental income – and he has dramatically reduced his risk of failure because he can draw on three decades of commercial experience running businesses for profit.

He also diversifies risk by continuing to support cleantech businesses in order to generate income to afford the renovations, but also because he wants to keep involved with industry and use his experience to progress the energy transition.

Kia, the Purpose Coach & Intuitive Artist

Kia did a range of jobs she didn't enjoy as an executive assistant in a range of sectors she didn't enjoy either. In her heart she was an artist, a creative, but the corporate jobs paid well and suited her whilst her husband was building his brand and design consultancy.

Until they took too much toll on her physically and emotionally.

With more stability at home, children starting school, Kia found she had more time. She decided it was her moment. She enrolled in an art course at her local community centre, exhibited her paintings and began to create a following on Instagram and selling her paintings through Etsy.

But Kia was also driven by the need to help others unlock their creative passions. She wrote an e-book, sharing her experience and method of building a creative-based business, which she promoted on Instagram and Etsy. She received a lucky break getting a promotion through Moo, the printing company... over night she had thousands of e-book downloads, giving her a passive income (revenue that takes negligible effort to acquire) and generating over 23,000 followers.

Kia has since used her following to build a community, with a membership subscription, coaching people online to find their purpose, build their confidence and nurture their creativity. She attracts people from all over the world to join her courses, which she runs from her living room at home.

Today, she is running an advanced Intuitive Artist course just for experienced artists who have been on the journey with her for several years.

In addition, Kia writes a monthly feature in a magazine and is part-way through a book on listening to your intuition.

Follow Kia @kiacannons or visit kiacannons.com.

You can hear more of Kia's story on the Corporate Escapology podcast.

Practical inspiration

There's no shortage of people on Instagram, TikTok and LinkedIn if you're looking for a formula for making six- or even seven-digit incomes, often entirely passively. Most are selling the modern-day equivalent of snake oil, because making money online is hard. And most agree, it's harder than it used to be – but it's still an opportunity, and a low risk one at that.

Kia puts her success down to aligning passion and purpose with a gap in the market. She is clear about her target audience, their pains and needs, and she offers a creative community, with support, structure and accountability.

Kia's large following enables her to quickly test her offers, as well as sell products to a community of like-minded people.

She makes her various purpose-led businesses work around her family and her home, keeping her costs low and with a singular focus on where she can help her community thrive.

Lilli, going independent with purpose

Lilli is a design consultant, specializing in service design. She spent a decade or more working in corporate innovation and design working both in-house and consulting. In 2020, she refocused on design for climate change, and specifically climate resilience and adaptation, helping businesses prepare for extreme weather, risks and other types of disruption. She negotiated a four day week with a new consultancy, leaving her a day each week to freelance and run workshops for businesses concerned about climate resilience.

Over the next couple of years, Lilli built up enough business to stop her consultancy job and now works full-time as a freelancer serving multiple clients. Lilli has recognized that working freelance is one of the best ways to build her own resilience and adapt to potential disruptions – since she can work for whomever, wherever and whenever she chooses.
To support and provide advice to other freelancers focused on climate and social change, as well as share freelancing opportunities, Lilli has built a community of solopreneurs and freelancers called IMMA Collective – for Impact Makers.

Follow Lilli on LinkedIn (search: Elisabeth Graf) or visit immacollective.com.

You can hear more of Lilli's story on the Corporate Escapology podcast.

 Practical inspiration
Lilli de-risked her move to independent consulting by negotiating a four day week, buying her time to build her client base and refine her offer. She actually took a Friday one week and the Monday the next week, giving her a block of four days to focus. She was careful to avoid conflicts of interest by targeting different client profiles in different countries.

Lilli stepped back from her own challenge of going independent to think more strategically about her differentiated offer and how she could help others. This opened up the opportunity for IMMA Collective, another source of revenue, as well as network and authority.

To read more inspiring stories of people who have escaped corporate life to build more fulfilling lives visit corporateescapology.com/stories.

Spectrums of possibilities

There you are. Twelve ideas to consider after you leave your corporate job. But do note, each one of them is a spectrum of possibilities, not a single box with just one binary option inside, yes or no.

Don't think 'I couldn't sell online courses, like Kia', '... be a coach like Erica' or 'I have no idea how to make beautiful ceramics like Steve'.

Their stories are illustrative.

As I've said, coaching, for instance, takes multiple forms: individual to group, programme-based with a single goal, domain-specific coaching or executive coaching. Coaching bleeds into mentoring and even close to therapy (though maybe it shouldn't).

Freelancing can cover anything from by-the-hour advice or projects, to effectively 'body-shopping' for longer periods of time for companies who lack your skills.

Startups can be software, hardware, data or knowledge-based, targeting consumers or other businesses – they are in every industry, some with a profit motive, some not. You can join as a co-founder, advisor, employee, freelancer, mentor. The support and value you can add with your corporate experience is limitless.

And lastly, consultants – they can usually do, and be, anything you want. They cover a spectrum from the smart generalist who can turn their hand to most things, to a technical specialist who might do fewer, higher fee hours for a narrow field of clients. Other consultants might write reports all day from home.

The point is there is a myriad of options, each with broad spectrums, for you to consider.

Don't jump to the easy or obvious one, or the one everyone expects or tells you you'll be good at. Consider your North Star and your goals – and experiment.

A word about portfolio careers

They're all the rage these days, for everyone from Gen Z on the beach to the Silver Surfers topping up pensions. They couldn't be more different from the traditional corporate career, where you do one thing full time, all year, every year, your whole life.

A portfolio career is one made up of multiple sources of income with no single employer. The emerging 'gig economy' has rightfully received bad press, owing to abuse of zero-hours contracts for lower paid workers. But it has also opened up opportunities for some people to make money, with more flexibility than with a full-time job.

Like driving for Uber, letting a room through Airbnb, offering creative services through Fiverr or Upwork. A whole entrepreneurial world associated with Amazon, Instagram, TikTok and other platforms is enabling thousands of people to ditch their jobs and retire early. At least that's what they say.

My favourite book on the subject of portfolio careers is *The Multi-Hyphen Method* by Emma Gannon. Emma is a Corporate Escapologist herself, having exited a very successful career in PR to go it alone, specifically to write. In *The Multi-Hyphen Method* she talks about the 'Hyphens' or gigs that she undertook to bring in the cash that enabled her to dedicate time to write.

Emma is an advocate of this way of working: 'It's essentially about being a happier person at work, but it also has economic business sense behind it.'

Now with ten books behind her, Emma continues to lead a Multi-Hyphen career as a coach, runs retreats and writes on Substack, where she now earns a 'six-figure' income.

Dayna's story

Dayna successfully navigated a career within the pharmaceuticals industry, with a mix of corporate and consulting jobs over an 18-year period. When her employer announced a major restructuring within a year of her joining, she knew she would not be entitled to any redundancy pay-out and decided she would leave rather than face months of uncertainty.

Dayna and I worked through an audit of her skills, experience and know-how (see Chapter 5). She recognized that she had a broad enough range of skills to set up by herself as a consultant and sell services to her former employers.

Dayna had retained good relationships with her previous companies, as well as with colleagues who had moved on, several into consultancy. She was able to test some of her hypotheses about the type of work, contracting and pricing with them during her notice period, thereby reducing the risk of a failed 'launch'. As she left, she secured a small piece of consultancy from a previous employer to get her started.

Dayna took the decision to limit consultancy to three days a week, leaving her two days to explore a new passion she had developed during the lockdowns of teaching yoga. She ran classes online for two mornings a week and built a following during her first year. During her second year, Dayna continued the consultancy and yoga, and also set up a new e-commerce business selling clothes and other products related to yoga.

Dayna has diversified her income streams, turned passions into businesses and continues to develop her corporate capabilities, ensuring she remains in demand for her pharmaceutical clients.

A word about careers

For many of you that have spent a long time climbing a corporate career ladder, it can be daunting to think 'What next?'

I'm not sure I really considered myself as having a career when I was at BP, it felt more like a series of jobs that I mostly enjoyed, in which I learnt something and got paid.

But perhaps if you have systematically worked your way up from junior roles through management and into executive positions it may feel like a career.

And moving away from this may feel like you're giving all that up.

It might be a good time to probe a little deeper into this career of yours:

o What's its purpose and where's it heading?

o Is it still giving you what you need?

o How much more has it got to give?

Answering these questions might be revealing.

I think these days, especially when we've invested so much time in building capabilities that others value, we can afford to be a bit more fluid, or 'squiggly' as Helen Tupper and Sarah Ellis refer to it in their book *The Squiggly Career*. Although the book is geared towards people inside the corporate, it may count even more outside.

In many ways, harnessing everything you've learnt and have become, to design a life that fits around you, and gives you purpose and meaning, may be the crowning achievement of any career.

There's no sunk cost because the value is leaving with you. Let's face it, there are fewer options open to you now at your level, with competition from a new generation coming up behind. The big leadership role may never come your way. Worse, your career may be plateauing. But that doesn't mean it needs to end here.

Quite the reverse. The next stage, beyond your corporate career, may be your best yet.

Ideas and options

You've read some inspiring stories of other Corporate Escapologists, you've learnt more about portfolio careers and you may have begun to challenge some of your beliefs about the need for a career.

Now I want you to jot down some ideas of things that have piqued your interest. Or ideas you already have for what you might do next.

_____

_____

_____

_____

_____

_____

_____

Don't do any filtering or censoring. Don't think about what's possible. Or whether you have the right capabilities or the confidence or the network.

Only think about what you want.

Also, don't fixate on one idea. List as many as you can. Firstly, because you can try all of them if you choose. And secondly, because you may find where you eventually land is a blend of more than one. And thirdly, because that blend may make you stand out.

Now look at this list. Where are you drawn? What ideas do you like? Which ideas play to your strengths and where your energy lies? In my experience, you usually have more than an inkling.

Let's give these ideas a bit of a kick now, shall we? To test them against some of the things, the 'Fit Factors', that you've already decided are important – OKRs, Capabilities, Energizers, Constraints.

Let's now take a look at Exercise 14.

Exercise 14: Idea Validation

Exercise instructions

Step 1   Write down your top three ideas and see how well they match with the OKRs you set out earlier in the book. Mark them High, Medium or Low. Do these ideas allow or enable these things? Or is there a gap – or an incompatibility?

Step 2   Now do the same for each idea against the Capabilities you identified in Part II – your skills, experience, know-how and strengths (again, High, Medium or Low).

Do your ideas take advantage of the unique blend of capabilities that make you special? Or are there gaps? Maybe you can close these gaps with some training, education or experience? Or are you deluding yourself about something that you know in your heart that you won't ever do?

Step 3   Next, evaluate each of your ideas (High/Medium/Low) for how it energizes you – you'll know if the idea fills you with excitement, dread or ambivalence. You have an opportunity to be 'in flow' a lot more often than you are today. You might even get that jump-out-of-bed feeling where your energy levels are much higher than today.

Step 4   Finally, test these ideas against some of the realities or constraints you identified in Chapter 6, particularly affordability and predictability. Mark them High, Medium or Low.

Don't worry if many of your ideas don't fit well with some of your Fit Factors – you'll identify ways to close gaps in Part IV. For now, focus on your ambition and what feels exciting to you.

Idea Validation

I like the sound of

OKRs

Capabilities

Energizers

Financials

Over the next few days keep flicking back to this page. How does it make you feel? You'll quickly realize some feel more right than others.

You might want to test them out with other people. See what they think. Take their advice on board, but this is about you.

Now add the ideas that excite you to your Escape Plan Canvas in the Appendix, under 'Ideas I want to explore'. Just for a record and to keep you moving forward.

That's Part III complete, the Explore phase of the Escape Method. Part IV is up next, which is all about the exit itself.

Chapter summary

o Making a significant change creates opportunities to try new things and experiment practically before committing. But incremental changes can also do you good – it doesn't all need to be a big transformation or pivot.

o Failed experiments will teach you as much, if not more, than the successful experiments – and both will teach you more than imagining what might happen.

o Other people's stories can inspire confidence and generate ideas that you can copy or learn from.

o Portfolio careers are all the rage for good reason, because they enable variety and flexibility – two things that are challenging to find in a corporate job.

o The idea of a career is more fluid today than in the past and is simply a label which you may choose to embrace or reject.

IV Exit corporate life

We've now passed the mid-point where things may start to feel a bit more real now, where you'll need to come out, so to speak, about this new you. Up until now, it may well have been a covert operation – getting into the right mindset, gradually detaching from your corporate life, objectively evaluating your skills and experiences and opening your mind to new possibilities.

I hope it hasn't been too covert, because it's good to share this journey with others, especially close family and friends, because they can support and encourage you. And because they are important stakeholders in your success.

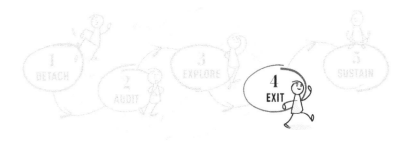

Part IV of the Escape Method is all about the Exit itself. When you need to take everything out of your head – and hopefully out of the notes you've scribbled – and make it real.

In Chapter 9 you will consider your new identity and how to reposition yourself for your new life. In Chapter 10, you will build strategies and new capabilities to help you get started in this new life and increase your chances of success. In Chapter 11, you will identify gaps or areas that require further work which might impact you reaching your goals and North Star. Finally, in Chapter 12, The Great Escape, you're going to pull everything together into a simple plan that provides focus and momentum.

There's a lot to do, so let's get started.

CHAPTER 9

Repositioning yourself

'To handle yourself, use your head; to handle others, use your heart.'

Eleanor Roosevelt, Reformer

Let's start with identity. Remember in Part I, I talked about how you'll have to unpick some of your corporate identity, the parts that are bound up in who you work for? Obviously, you can no longer say you work for someone when you don't – although I have seen people keep their former employer on their LinkedIn for months, even years, which is odd.

I recommend a clean break.

But to what?

Who are you now?

Or who will you be, without that household name attached to you?

I've said before how I found relief in awkward social gatherings when I could simply answer 'I work for BP' when asked what I did for a living.

Not having that simple answer hasn't been easy, I'll admit.

For the first year or two I tried various things from 'I work for myself' to 'I'm a marketing consultant' to 'I work with startups' to the very vague 'Lots of things'. Often we just want the person to find someone else to make small talk with and a quick fob-off is all that's required.

But if you continue to do this, you potentially miss out on the chance to tell people what you do, and therefore miss opportunities for new business.

Added to which, there's always a risk that unless you are crystal clear about your identity, someone else will define it for you, e.g. 'He used to work for BP, but now he always seems to be in the reduced section at the garden centre.'

It's time to become a bit more deliberate, a bit more intentional about your identity, so you can use it to your advantage.

I recommend three statements of varying lengths that describe what you will do once you have left:

1   The Fob-off – you need it, you might as well make it useful.

2   The Interest-Piquer – once useful for elevators, now for Zoom.

3   The Pitch – what, how, impact.

Before you get going, flick back to your goals in Chapter 7, and your SEKSE canvas in Chapter 5. These should inform your identity and how you talk about yourself. They need to be authentic. Too much marketing spin and you sound daft: 'Content Visionary' was a real job title I was given once, but never embraced. Too little spin and people doze off. Also, there needs to be some aspiration in here – project forward six months to a year and imagine how you're talking about yourself then.

These are mine to give you an idea:

1   The Fob-off

    I work with corporates and startups mainly in the clean energy space.

2   The Interest-Piquer

I help startups, corporates and academics innovate together to solve problems that neither one could solve alone.

3   The Pitch

I bring together startups, corporates and academics to innovate, build and scale technology businesses. Through mentoring, workshops and structured support, I help all sides solve problems they couldn't solve alone.

I've also got another three for the other side of my working life, Corporate Escapology:

1   The Fob-off

I help people who want to leave corporate life prepare for what's next.

2   The Interest-Piquer

I help people who are stuck in jobs that no longer serve them to build the confidence and the capabilities to leave, without taking unnecessary risks.

3   The Pitch

Most people in corporate jobs eventually begin to wonder what else they could do. I coach those looking to leave to prepare for exit, helping them to develop the right mindset, objectively evaluate their skills and offer and explore new possibilities. Then I help them build an Escape Plan so they exit and land safely.

Now it's your turn (see Exercise 15).

Exercise 15: Identity Statement

Exercise instructions

Step 1	Start by writing your one line Fob-off for people you barely know, e.g. at a school event or when bumping into a former colleague.
Step 2	Next, draft your Interest-Piquer, using language that refers to your customer's problem, hinting at your solution. Try to make it just one line if you can, I'll allow a subordinate clause.

Step 3   Finally, write your Pitch – no more than 20
seconds. Your Pitch needs to set out your stall with
confidence and a bit of verve.

Make sure there's consistency between each of them and try to
make them rock solid.

Identity Statement

The fob-off

The interest piquer

The pitch

Experiment time

Now, you've got to start testing them out. First out loud to
yourself, then in front of a mirror, then in front of people you
like. And eventually in front of people you don't know.

What kind of reaction do you get? Puzzled looks? Hasty exits?
Or more questions? You'll be surprised how many times you'll
hear: 'Oh you should speak to my friend…' as the lines start
to work.

Test them out for a week or two, until you build confidence that they fly.

Then start using them – social channels, websites, email reach-outs.

One word

I'm sorry to report that although you can use these identity statements for most interactions with people, you will need a one- or two-word description to sum yourself up – mainly for application forms, but also sometimes for events and the odd formal thing.

It's annoying and reductive. But you need to get comfortable with it.

You've probably heard the Brené Brown TED talk when she describes defining herself at a conference as a Researcher-Storyteller. She made up the term, so she retained the academic component, even though it sounded a bit silly.

Tim Ferris wrote in the 4-Hour Week:

> I never enjoyed answering this cocktail question because it reflects an epidemic I was long part of: job descriptions as self-descriptions. If someone asks me now and is anything but absolutely sincere, I explain my lifestyle of mysterious means simply. 'I'm a drug dealer.' Pretty much a conversation ender.

Whatever works for you – but don't sound silly. Or illegal.

You might as well think about it now.

I tend to use 'consultant'. It's bland enough that it fobs most people and forms off but is still fairly substantive and serious. I use 'coach' as well for some clients.

Find a word you're comfortable with. And keep practising it until it feels normal and you don't feel so self-conscious.

It's actually a bigger deal than you might imagine because for the first time it's just describing you, not some bigger entity that gave you protection from annoying questions. You're more vulnerable now, which is a good and bad thing. So invest some time in doing this.

The penultimate box in the Escape Plan Canvas, in the Appendix, has a gap for you to add one or two possible new identities you've developed, drop them in there now.

The bits that never go away – and you may not want them to

In Part I, I talked about the great things we gain from our corporate careers – rewards, status, stability – and particularly development.

And that development, converted into more discrete, tangible skills, experience and know-how, travels with you. It doesn't remain in the corporate. Your value to them pretty much dries up the day you walk out the door. But their value to you continues. Which is very useful.

I just wouldn't recommend incorporating your old employer in your new identity. It's time for the butterfly to emerge.

Even if you choose to reposition yourself into something totally different from your corporate career, like Martin upping sticks moving to the Lake District to build a holiday lettings business, you carry your lived experiences and learning with you.

Arnab's story

Arnab (not his real name) studied law and went on to qualify in a Magic Circle firm in London as a commercial property solicitor. From the start he hated the hours but was swept up by being told how well he was doing. He admits now he craved too much external validation at the expense of how he really felt inside – but he gave little time to those internal feelings because he was so busy.

Over time, Arnab married, had two children and ploughed on as the chief breadwinner – he felt an overwhelming and acute sense of responsibility.

But by then he had built a name for himself in a niche field of commercial property. He was invited to talk at small conferences, actively participated in new business calls and was engaged by other firms to provide technical advice.

Arnab gradually became aware that his knowledge was valuable and could potentially create an income stream outside his job, selling his experience and advice to multiple law firms and corporate property clients.

He set himself a goal of leaving his firm within 12 months, using the time to prepare. He developed and tested his offer, created marketing materials (a website and PDF brochure) and started to build his network.

With a few trusted advisors he gathered feedback on his new career path and sought out referrals.

Nine months into his 12-month plan, his law firm merged with another. Rumours of job cuts circulated and Arnab was decisive, handing in his notice to begin his new career.

Arnab was ready; he'd got clear about his customer, his offer and his new identity. Within weeks he had taken on several new clients and within a year had a small team of associates supporting his business to grow.

Whilst the world is almost your oyster when you've built a corporate career, and you have the option to pivot to something really different, most people tend to 'evolve' rather than walk away from everything and start again.

Because there's usually no need – and far more to gain from bringing your skills, experience and know-how with you.

My advice would be to build on who you are today, what you know and can do. Don't feel like you need to exit to a completely new you. It's an unnecessary risk.

It implies what went before wasn't valuable or useful. And I don't believe that.

Validation

The last part of this chapter is about avoiding delusion, hearing what you want to hear and the dreaded Confirmation Bias, where you only look for the nodding heads and smiles and discount the rest.

It's time to start asking people for feedback. Maybe you have already tested your new identity, so build on this.

Share your Escape Plan Canvas (see the Appendix) with nice people you know, who will be honest but not tear apart every shred of your confidence. Then go wider with your network – a coach, a colleague, a client. Each time refining and adjusting your Canvas, your story, your answers to their questions.

And try to end by asking them how they might support you.

A word about feedback
Taking on feedback can be tough. You make yourself vulnerable, offering yourself up for a bit of an emotional kicking. But without it, you're shooting in the dark, running the risk of a much bigger, and maybe costlier, kicking. Far better now to sit with a bit of vulnerability. And remember for every constructive point, you will hear lots of positive feedback, so embrace it.

Here are three tips when gathering feedback:

1   Most of us are predisposed to hear only negative feedback, so make sure you also actively listen for the positive comments.

2   Be wary about single data points – always look for more people giving consistent feedback before making any changes.

3   People are people and they have their own agenda, they live in their own worlds and they may not really understand what you're trying to achieve and why. They may try to steer you towards something that's not for you. I have a nodding smile for these kinds of conversations where I'm thinking 'No, that's more about you'.

Be brave. Like Churchill wrote: 'Criticism may not be agreeable, but it is necessary. It fulfils the same function as pain in the human body. It calls attention to an unhealthy state of things.'

Chapter summary

o   Define a new identity – or experiment with several.

o   Make sure you have something for the awkward moments when you need to explain who you are and what you do.

o   If you're clear about what you do and where you need help, most people will bend over backwards to help.

o   You won't lose your old corporate identity when you leave – in most cases it will create value for you and open doors long after.

CHAPTER 10

New networking

'Courage starts with showing up and letting ourselves be seen.'
Brené Brown, Professor & Writer

I left my corporate job with 650 connections on LinkedIn.

When I scanned through them, more than 80% worked at BP. It was a pretty insular network. But I wasn't unique then – and I don't believe I am today.

You 'network' with the people who can help you get most things done. Inside a corporate, that's other corporate employees. Unless you're in sales or maybe procurement. But in most big companies that's actually a small proportion of the workforce.

Most people are feeding the machine from the inside.

Outside the circle

Once you leave the company you're no longer inside the circle. You can no longer access internal systems or the people inside. Sure, people are polite, but you're no longer someone of influence. To be fair, you can't help them like you once did.

This can reinforce any rejection you're already feeling: isolation, disconnection, discombobulation. It can leave you especially vulnerable if you are planning to make your living through your old corporate networks.

The practical things you can do here are pretty obvious:

1   Spam everyone you know to tell them you've left and what you're planning to do next.

2   Go on a frenzy of LinkedIn self-promotion to connect with as many people as possible

3   Pitch up at a load of networking events and pray someone wants to engage.

Today, the hotels where networking takes place have been replaced by Zoom. It's BYO and you can sneak out without even having to excuse yourself. End call, I've had enough.

Or you can meet one-on-one, which is far and away my preferred networking *modus operandi*.

One of the great things about working more remotely these days is it's low risk for two people to 'network', i.e. have a call.

Compare it with meeting someone for coffee in real life: book something a few days, or even weeks, in advance, hope the place you've booked is conducive to the kind of meeting you want and pray that your new friend shows up and doesn't get a better offer. You could easily find yourself wasting an afternoon and a chunk of change on a train fare and designer coffees.

Now it's much easier. Tools like Calendly take out the frustration of finding a time that works for both of you and Zoom happily records and transcribes your conversations so you don't even have to worry about taking notes.

So there really are no excuses.

And for those who just want to dip their toe in, there's LinkedIn, Facebook groups and an online community for every niche under the sun.

Other technologies can help you increase your network fast. One of my gigs is with Startupbootcamp, where I run a startup accelerator programme. When I was scouting for startups, the team set up an automated 'reach-out' using a tool called Dripify with a semi-personalized message from me, based on some relevant criteria in a LinkedIn profile.

My network of cleantech startups and venture capitalists was expanding 25+ a day, which mounts up fast – due to network effects.

Useful for that particular gig, but admittedly not much use for this book.

The point is, if you want numbers, you can get them.

But it's pretty shallow. Quantity over quality.

It's scattergun marketing and I'm not a fan. I want my marketing to feel more thoughtful, more special. Like I care about the individual and am invested in the relationship. What problem is someone facing – and can I help them?

You would be amazed how productive connecting with just a few people, with intention, each week can be – and how much easier it is on the ego too.

Don't dilute yourself.

Now it's time for Exercise 16.

Exercise 16: Work The Network

Exercise instructions

| Step 1 | You're likely to need a few different networks after you exit corporate life – especially if, like me, you want to try out multiple paths. Give each one a name – and add it to one of the boxes on the right. |
| Step 2 | Then add a few names in the ovals of the people or companies that might be able to help you move in those circles and become part of that network. |

If you need more nodes for your network, all the exercises and templates are free to download at corporateescapology.com/tools.

For Corporate Escapology, I had three target audiences: outplacement organizations, business and career coaches and HR directors of medium-sized companies. I put each one in the right-hand-side boxes and then thought of everyone I knew who might be able to help me talk to someone in those organizations. I knew quite a lot of coaches so that was easy, a few medium-sized companies, so I could reach their HR directors.

Work The Network

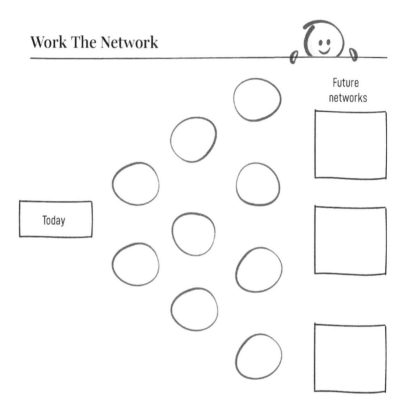

But I knew no-one other than the outplacement consultant who helped me when I left my job and she had moved on. So I had to build a network from scratch.

Except it's never from scratch. Everyone is six degrees of separation from someone else. With LinkedIn maybe it's only three.

Who can help you build new networks? How can you reduce the number of nodes and move faster? Can you try multiple routes?

Start now

Recall the Chinese proverb:

> *The best time to plant a tree was 20 years ago. The second best time is now.*

It's the same with networking. Start today. If you haven't already left your corporate job, for goodness' sake start before you leave. Use your preferred social media channel, reach out to people over email, go to events if that's your thing.

You'll often find it easier to do this as a corporate employee – there's often more perceived incentive for others to connect with you. But not always, sometimes it generates confusion, so give it some thought which persona you use – current or future. This sort of thing presents an excellent opportunity to practise your new identity, so try it out.

Something I really recommend with clients who don't plan to jump imminently is to expand their networks by giving their time to something *pro bono*, i.e. free of charge.

Whether that's sitting on a board, advising a charity, mentoring a startup, providing training or coaching or maybe offering your (future) services in test-mode. Your corporate credentials will undoubtedly help here. And your network is likely to grow alongside your confidence. You will also be able to test and gather feedback to validate demand for your post-move pathway.

It's part of your de-risking strategy, exploring and building the foundations on which to base your move.

Just don't be a taker. It's number one of my rules for networking.

Rule Number 1: Give First

During my last couple of years at BP, I worked with two brilliant entrepreneurs at the venture-builder we set up, John Mushriqui and Illai Gescheit. They taught me something that has changed my life forever: Give First: how can I help you? This is my Rule Number 1 in networking. It's how things work in the startup world. But it's really not like that in a corporate, even a nice one. There, everyone has plans, objectives, functional boundaries, even timesheets, so few people go out of their way. The ones who do stand out.

Give First is a game-changer in networking. It builds a strong network of people clamouring to reciprocate over time.

And 'over time' is important because it's not about building transactional relationships where you have to give and receive every time you meet; the giving and receiving can happen over months and even years.

There are some people who only want to give, probably because they've received so much over the years.

Years later, after leaving my corporate job, I really notice it in most of my conversations with non-corporate people. It comes over naturally, genuinely and it encourages the person on the other side to reciprocate. We actually become better versions of ourselves in situations that would ordinarily be quite awkward.

Just try it.

Super-connectors

Another phenomenon you come across when you've left corporate life is the super-connector. The person who seems to know everyone. Super-connectors understand that their value comes from introducing people to other people. They don't hold their black books close to their chests, they share the contents – but wisely. They don't want to introduce people who will harm their own reputation. They understand that their intrinsic value lies in vetting for quality and relevance. And filtering out the takers.

Bad super-connectors just make introductions like 'Thought you two should meet'. Good ones make personal introductions. They describe how they think you will both benefit from the relationship and they coach you how.

Lucy Werner is one of those good super-connectors. She's the author of the highly recommended book *Hype Yourself* and runs a paid community on Substack (hypeyourself.substack.com).

She loves nothing more than connecting people and has done wonders for my network, pairing me up with podcast guests and shows, guest blogs, not to mention media opportunities. Find your Lucy, or just find Lucy.

There's a great Harvard Business Review from 2005 about 'Brokers' [How to build your network, Brian Uzzi/Shannon Dunlop] – Brokers is just another word for super-connector. The authors advise, 'To build a network rich in social capital, cultivate powerful brokers who aren't in positions of formal authority.'

The last part is important about seeking out those without formal authority, so you're not knocking on the same doors as everyone else.

If you have a good network you might set yourself up as a super-connector. Several people I know have done just this, leveraging their huge networks of people in and outside their former company.

The key is relevance. Don't waste anyone's time. Focus on the value someone else gains by having you as another node in their network.

One fellow Corporate Escapologist, Andy, told me how his old corporate network had helped him since he left. He works on a contract basis for a huge multi-national based in Asia which is growing fast and needs high-quality, self-reliant talent. My friend has done a good job keeping in touch with former colleagues and is now connecting them to new opportunities – he knows what his client needs and which of his former colleagues would add value (and which would not).

You don't have to work very hard to find super-connectors. In my experience, they end up finding you.

Rule Number 2: Be clear

Rule number 2 about networking is almost the opposite of Give First: you must be able to communicate where you need help.

Most people like helping other people. They get a buzz out of it. But all too often they can't help because they don't know how. Because the other person isn't clear what they need.

You need to be specific. Make it easy for someone else to help you.

In the next chapter you're going to look at the gaps you need to close before you exit your corporate job. Being able to translate these gaps into requests for help will save you a lot of time and help you build relationships with the people helping you.

Try it out. See how being clear about what you want opens things up.

Just remember: Give First – your job is also to help others.

Build your squad

I love the idea of network effects. You really see it happening as you start getting out and talking to people. Invariably the conversation will end with a 'You should talk with…' moment, where the other person will effectively offer up a node in their network to join yours. And if the moment doesn't arrive, make it happen – 'Who do you think I should speak with next?' or, even better, 'Is there anyone else you think I could help?'.

The term 'tribe' is over-used these days, but get past the cliché and it's a worthy concept – find the people with similar or complementary ideas (or even different ones), the people on the same mission, etc. Finding those people as fast as possible can really help validate your hypotheses about your next chapter – and give you wings to accelerate progress.

Beth Stallwood, author of WorkJoy, was on Alison Jones' brilliant *Extraordinary Business Book Club* podcast, episode 356 (!), talking about the squad of people she advocates building when starting anything new. Find a Cheerleader, Challenger, Comrade, Creator, Connector and Conjuror. Each archetype provides something you need to help you through the change. I love the concept, but don't worry – you don't need them all in place before you start, two people may help perform more than one role and you may need different people at different times anyway. Collectively, your squad helps you become better, they challenge you but with kindness and support, willing you on to success.

Although your squad is powerful, it's just one super-node in your network – don't let it become the only one. Not only because you can get pretty insular talking to the echo-chamber, but more importantly because diversity opens you up to all manner of opportunities. Let people around you see connections and opportunities that you don't see yourself.

I mentioned earlier that I did a podcast for my friend Erica, and before it aired, I got an email from another of her guests, Yael Iffergan. She is a head-hunter in the US. Like I suspect many people, I am a bit wary of recruiters – 'I'm not looking for a job' I emailed when she reached out.

But it turned out Yael wanted to speak to me because she liked the sound of Corporate Escapology and wanted to know more, but mainly because she has clients who are not yet ready to leave their corporate jobs, even if they say they are – and she thought she could refer those people to me for help (and then pick them up later when they were ready for recruitment).

And because of my false stereotyping, I might have missed this opportunity for us to help one another. Yael also introduced me to another contact, Jon, who I interviewed as part of my research for this book – Yael is a super-connector.

People are often thinking about how you can be useful to them. Which has perils but also potential. Networks help you access the potential; boundaries help you avoid the perils.

A final word about networking. I don't mind admitting I hate the face-to-face kind. I loathe going into rooms full of strangers. Or making polite chit chat.

But now in my very late 40s, I focus on super-charging my strengths – not trying to get average at my weaknesses.

I'm good one-on-one, I'm good on Zoom, I'm helpful and I'm curious – so that's the kind of networking I do.

For you it might be different. You might want to ease yourself into things, with a set number of hours you commit to 'do networking', or the kind of help you offer, so you don't feel overwhelmed or trapped by a taker. One of my friends said she'd learnt how to deliver a 'Nice no'.

Boundaries are important, but don't simply avoid the things that make you uncomfortable, because that's how you will grow.

Instead, find what works for you and do more of that.

Do you like sales?

One of the things that invariably comes up in my conversations with would-be Corporate Escapologists is selling. Or, rather, fear of selling or being bad at selling.

It's something with which I identify.

Many of us carry stereotypes of pushy or aggressive salespeople selling timeshares, used cars, insurance, charity, your next home. Like me, you might think 'If that is selling, I can't do it'. The thought of pitching in front of a boardroom of suits makes my heart race. And not in a good way.

These examples are caricatures, of course. They persist because they contain some truth. But they're not the whole truth. And they're not where you need to be.

My fear of selling was one of the things that made me leave consulting before joining BP. I sneaked out the grade before you were set a sales target.

At BP I became the client.

I was much better at buying than selling.

But I hate someone smarming up to me and trying to flog me something.

Only three times in 20 years did I run a pitch to find an agency or partner to deliver something for me. And only once would I say it was successful.

The rest of the time I built relationships. One person at a time. I went into a potential partner's office, to meet them on their home turf, casually over a coffee. I politely stopped them midway through their credentials deck and tried to get to know them as people I might like to work with.

So why should it be any different now I'm on the other side?

Of course, there are clients who want the grand pitch, the big idea with the big reveal (for free), to be wined and dined, to have their ego massaged.

But they're not my kind of clients.

And they don't need to be yours. Unless you like that kind of thing.

Two things I have learnt over the last few years stop me freaking out over sales or fearing I'm going to need to become something I'm not.

And both play to our corporate advantages:

1   Selling is a whole lot easier if you find the right customer for you – and you build a relationship with them. You can call it selling if you want. Or helping. Or solving problems. Because that's the kind of selling that experienced people like us do best, problem-solving.

2   Selling is not a single thing, but rather a bunch of interactions and behaviours – and we corporate people often tend to be really good at them (see Chapter 5, Exercise 7: Six Prisms).

To get on in corporate life you can't not be a salesperson. Persuading people. Understanding stakeholders. Handling objections. Storytelling. Even the deeply technical wizards I worked with in BP's technology function quickly realized they lost budget if they couldn't sell their ideas to more senior leaders.

Fear of being bad at selling is one of those Bad Thinking barriers (see Chapter 3) that can actually stop people who want to leave from going through with it. It's that big. I guess it's because of both fear of the humiliation of failing and fear of the consequences of failing, i.e. no income.

As with all Bad Thinking, the only solution is to flip it, turn it on its head and support Good Thinking with logic, e.g.:

1   Most of you won't humiliate yourself selling in front of a big group because that won't be the kind of selling you do (maybe ever).

2   If you don't win some work with a client, the opportunity just fades away – it doesn't get announced on LinkedIn – no-one knows.

3   You have highly developed skills to successfully build relationships, which are the bedrock of sales.

You're actually a natural at selling. Except in truth it hasn't really come naturally. Like many things you now do, you've learnt these skills during your corporate career, you've honed your strengths, you've proven your experience.

You're going to be ok.

Chapter summary

○   Your network needs to change as your corporate network will become less useful. Ideally, begin growing this before you leave your job.

○   Be intentional about who you want to connect with and why, rather than make indiscriminate attempts to get your numbers up on LinkedIn.

○   Giving first, offering to help without expecting reciprocation, is a powerful way to build relationships, learn and gain experience.

○   Consider building a squad of trusted advisors around you who can provide different contributions when you need them most.

○   Get comfortable with selling. Your way of selling.

Mind the gap(s)

'Once we start to act, hope is everywhere. So instead of looking for hope, look for action. Then, and only then, hope will come.'

Greta Thunberg, Climate activist

The past ten chapters have focused on how brilliant you are and the incredible skills, experience and know-how you've picked up over the years.

But you may still have gaps that you need to fill.

In fact it's pretty likely that you will. Because you have spent many years learning to be successful in corporate life, you may have to unlearn some things and learn new things.

That's actually pretty exciting and is not to be feared. In most cases you have time.

Even if you have already left your corporate job and feel like the clock is ticking.

If you haven't yet left your corporate job, you are likely to have opportunities to close some of your gaps while continuing to work. The side-hustle might be one such route, where you test out your new future in your free time to learn what works, build a customer base and even earn some revenue.

Some people want to retrain and if they're lucky their current employer might even pay towards it. I knew one woman whose employer paid for her to go on a creative writing course, with time off to attend training – within a year she had left to write her best-selling novel. Clever.

A word about retraining

Sometimes it's necessary. You can't leave a job in marketing on a Friday and start on Monday in midwifery (thankfully) – you'll probably need to go back to university. That's a big deal, a huge (likely unpaid) commitment, but if that's your dream, plan for it and pursue it. I'm not talking about that kind of exit, where a qualification and the training that precedes it are legal requirements before you start a new job.

I'm talking about retraining to do a job that you're already experienced enough to do, but because of fear, or imposter syndrome, you use needing a qualification as the reason to defer getting on with it.

This is more common than you would think. I know because I've fallen into the trap several times: I decided I needed a Masters in Psychology because it would help me build a better customer discovery business. I decided I needed a coaching qualification because I wanted to coach people. I even toyed with doing a PhD in something to help me write this book.

Prevarication. Fear of failure. Anxiety around starting something new.

Could these qualifications have helped? Sure. But were they essential? Absolutely not.

If you want to leave your corporate career and retrain – fine, just make sure it's not because you think all your worries and anxieties about your competence will fade away. Because they won't. You'll still feel like an imposter even when you've got the certificate and the photo in the gown.

It's perfectly normal when we're doing something new.

Customers buying your services – as employers, consumers, clients, coachees, readers, partners, etc. – they confirm your competence and capability. There's no louder voice when it comes to validation than revenue. The sooner you get out practising what you know and how you can help others, the sooner you'll start feeling great.

And then it's unlikely that you'll ever think about going back to school. Although I still fancy that PhD.

Back to your gaps

Some gaps that block our exit are real, some are imagined. But in my experience, it's not worth brushing the ones that may be in your head under the carpet, because they tend to come back and bite you – or cause you untold angst at 3am when you can't sleep – and you're vulnerable to the gremlins.

Whether you're looking to leave your corporate job or have been made redundant, I find the Escape Method – Detach, Audit, Explore, Exit, Sustain – tends to surface most gaps. Typically, one stage makes you feel the most anxious and it's the one where you need to do most work.

Before you start working through your real or imagined gaps, I want to share some ideas about how you might close some of them. My aim is to open your mind to less conventional ways to close your gaps faster so that you can exit with a lower risk of landing unsafely and unsuccessfully.

Detach
This stage is all about unpicking what you value and will miss about corporate life. It's about being honest with yourself about why you want to leave and getting clear on what could lie ahead.

Common Detach gaps:

o   Lack of clarity around why you want to move.

o   Denial around what life will be like outside.

o   Unrealistic expectations.

o   Attachment to corporate identity and status.

Closing these gaps may require more one-to-one attention than a book can provide. You may need a coach to work through a blocker or to role-play different scenarios. You may even need a therapist to work through baggage you're carrying that's stopping you from moving forward.

One client I worked with had such low confidence that it was pointless progressing to the second stage, Audit – he needed professional support. Once he got that, we were able to work in parallel to get him out of the toxic work environment which was exacerbating his low self-esteem.

Other ways of closing gaps might be formalizing the time you take to work through priorities or needs. Some clients take an extended break, a sabbatical or go on a retreat to reset and establish what's important to them.

For others, it's enough to dedicate some time at home or on long walks to really identify what's holding you back.

It's a recurring theme of this book, but nothing quite helps you work through thorny problems like writing. It doesn't need to be journaling or Morning Pages, but write down how you're feeling, what you're expecting, what you're fearing... as soon as you've committed pen to paper your brain has a happy knack of helping you work out what to do next.

Audit

The exercises in this book may have highlighted that you don't know yourself as well as you thought, particularly the really good things. You may be undervaluing your skills, strengths and your contribution. This stage is also about helping you articulate your constraints, boundaries and future goals.

Common Audit gaps:

o   Shallow or biased view of self.

o   Lack of defined purpose or North Star.

o   Poor financial planning.

o   Insufficient stakeholder engagement.

o   Inadequate boundaries.

Actions to close these gaps could include psychometric profiling or working with specialist coaches who can evaluate you more objectively. Or they could be more focused on validating the profile you built for yourself in Part II with others – colleagues, mentors, family and friends, to reassure yourself that there are no overly positive or undue negative biases (more likely the latter).

If you skipped the work on your 360° profiling in Chapter 5, you should go back to this, otherwise you will short-change your escape.

Working with a coach can be helpful to build objectivity as well as to help set goals and understand your boundaries.

Actions to close gaps around financial planning might be investing in some budgeting software to build a really honest breakdown of your fixed costs and discretionary spending. Or you might want to work with a financial advisor.

Explore
Part III exposed you to some examples of the brave people who left their corporate careers to go on to build amazing lives that are serving them better. Remember each person sits on a spectrum of possible options that could be more or less right for you.

Common Explore gaps:

o Constrained, limited ideas.

o Discounting ideas too early without investigation or testing.

o Over confidence or rigid thinking about one idea.

o Limited experience or exposure to possible routes.

An action for you may be talking to people already doing something that interests you, maybe there's a community you can join or individuals you can meet via LinkedIn or Instagram who might share their experience.

You could listen to the Corporate Escapology podcast (plug!) where I talk to people who have left their corporate jobs to explore what they did next – and how it's worked out.

Maybe you want to actually try first-hand one of the options that's piqued your interest – to get some real-world experience – shadowing, work experience, a secondment.

Or maybe the action for you is a bigger experiment, like a side-hustle alongside the job, or a landing page with a bit of advertising spend to see if you get any takers for your product or service.

Exit

This stage of the Escape Plan is all about practical action, so it's likely it will have surfaced many of the gaps you see before you're ready to jump.

Common Exit gaps:

o   Vague or woolly identity.

o   Limited network or reluctance to expand it.

o   Capability gaps.

o   Prevarication.

Some of the exercises to define and practise your new identity may have kickstarted your efforts, but you may now need to get out into the real world. You may have actions to update your social profiles and any other digital channels, or to draft an introductory email or letter which you might want to try out.

Maybe you could experiment with some A/B testing where you try two different options in a small way and see which option works best before you scale up. This can be useful if, for example, you're investing in branding and marketing collateral.

I would be very surprised if you hadn't identified any gaps in your network, as you move from mostly internal corporate connections to the big wide world. Actions here may be about reaching out to people in your new network, asking to meet up, attending events, etc.

Devi's story

Devi worked in Employer Branding in Consumer Packaged Goods over a 15-year period for different companies. Over the years, she'd become frustrated and demotivated by low-impact projects and a growing resistance to change. But rather than leave, Devi embarked on a journey to study neuroscience at several pioneering institutes. She focused on organizational culture, peak performance, psychological safety and leadership. She threw herself into the data, really 'nerding out' as she put it.

She wrote papers and shared them with leaders in her company – way outside of her approved remit, her grade, her comfort zone. Soon, Devi was asked to conduct workshops for leadership teams, which snowballed into coaching hundreds of leaders. Invited back for regular check-ins, Devi became an accountability partner for these leaders. They loved her science-based approach to culture and the practical tools that could be implemented fast to adopt more desirable behaviours. Devi made herself vulnerable by collecting feedback on all her talks and workshops, as well as practising and refining her offer.

She ran this side-hustle consultancy inside the company for over three years, without financial reward, until one day, she said, 'I'm off; I can create more impact with my skills and expertise by being on the outside'.

Devi followed the Corporate Escapology model:

o   Detach: Over a three-year period, she saw that her company and career weren't serving her well and identified why and what needed to change.

o   Audit: She looked deep into herself and asked, 'What am I here for?', 'What do I do well?' and 'Where is the intersection between my passion and how I can help others?'

o   Explore: She was inspired by experts and academics in her field of interest but was more interested in applying the theory where she could have maximum impact on culture – with busy senior leaders.

o   Exit: She identified gaps in her knowledge and data, so she studied part-time. Later, she developed workshop products she could offer internal teams and then practised them to get better (actively seeking out feedback). She repositioned herself for a world outside, without taking a significant risk until she was ready to leap.

Now Devi's into Sustain.

She followed the advice of Paul Millerd in The Pathless Path, who uses the phrase 'prototype the leap' to describe how we can de-risk leaving our job by practising it in advance.

Devi may be a fearless leader, but her journey is open to all of us – whether we choose to get the qualifications or not. Learn and practise your craft before leaving, get feedback to improve your offer and shorten the distance you've got to leap to the other side.

Sustain

I haven't got here yet in the book, but I'm guessing you may well have identified some gaps in sticking to your plan.

Common Sustain gaps:

o   Commitment, sticking to something.

o   Looking back with rose-tinted glasses.

o   Plans B, C & D.

o   Support network.

Gaps like that support network, the back-up plan, conditions for a return, etc., all need some kind of action. Whether they need to be worked on before you leave or not, you can decide, but it's good to log them here.

Over the last few pages, you may have realized 'I'm not ready to make the jump just yet. I have work to do'. It's understandable. But just as what's measured gets managed, what's written down becomes actionable.

Now it's time for Exercise 17. For each stage of the Escape Method write down where you have a gap and what you're going to do about – and if it is really, really, truly stopping you from proceeding with your exit.

Or are you, just maybe, using it as an excuse to stay put?

Exercise 17: Mind The Gap(s)

Exercise instructions

Step 1	Write down the gaps you believe you have, particularly the ones you believe you need to close before you exit.
Step 2	Then define an action to close each gap. Maybe it's information, shadowing someone in a job, building a buffer, testing your business idea as a side-hustle. Write the action down.

Step 3   Now you need to be really honest with yourself: Does the action need to be complete before you're ready to exit? Is it a condition of exit? Is it an excuse? Or is it something you could complete after you've left?

Mark it High, Medium or Low.

Now take a hard Paddington Bear stare at what you've written down. What's really holding you back?

Mind The Gap(s)

Escape method stage	Gap	Actions to close	Dependency on exit plan
Detach			
Audit			
Explore			
Exit			
Sustain			

Hopefully that helped you get really practical about these gaps and also helped you prioritize the ones you have to deal with before you move, and the ones that can wait until after.

There's of course no science to this and once you start exiting, you're likely to identify other gaps you hadn't thought about. But I can also assure you that many of the gaps you thought you had before you left were less important than you had imagined.

For me, this is the classic 3am moment where I am worrying about something that is so catastrophic that I'm toying (for an hour or so) whether to get up and do something about it. Only to drift off and wake at 6am realizing the problem doesn't seem nearly so bad.

When you're on the precipice of exiting, it can feel like 3am all the time. But the other side is much more like 6am, infinitely more manageable and rarely solved by sleep-deprived catastrophizing.

In a short while, we'll transpose the gaps on which your exit is contingent into your Escape Plan, with the actions you're going to take to close them – and by when.

But first, if you haven't left your corporate job yet, there are some extra things you can do.

De-risk your exit from the inside

By far the best way to de-risk your exit from corporate life is to try some things out before you leave.

First things first, you need to be a bit careful here, as some companies stipulate in their employment contracts that you can only work for them. And if you're planning to do something that may compete with your current employer (even in adjacent markets or only tangentially) you need to be careful. Get legal advice. But if you're not sure, it might just be better not to try any side-hustles.

Some employment contracts have conditions about taking equity in other companies, if you're thinking about moonlighting for a startup, so again get legal advice.

But if you are free to experiment, do. What you do will depend on the options you have identified in Part III. Some of the escape stories there involved people running side-hustles while they were in their jobs. Partly to test demand, partly to refine their offer and partly to build confidence that they could generate revenue.

I've mentioned a few of these experiments before, but here's a reminder:

o   Set up a landing page with your services, supported by a few Google or Facebook ads, and see whether you get any signups.

o   Set up an e-commerce site to sell your product – or use Etsy or Shopify.

o   Coach or mentor – for free or in exchange for something.

o   Provide business advice to small companies in your local area.

o   Become a non-executive director.

o   Shadow someone or do work experience.

o   Write and publish your own content.

Each of these can be an experiment with a fixed duration and clear pass/fail metrics. Or they can be the first incarnation of the business you will grow once you have left your job.

Your biggest competition to running these experiments is time. You won't have much in the daytime and depending on your situation at home, you may not have much there either.

And this is why most people stay put.

Because they don't invest in the time to learn whether they should make the move. They don't build confidence in the move – or faith in themselves. And they don't refine their idea so it has the maximum chance of success.

Don't sabotage your move by being undisciplined, unfocused and uncommitted.

The success of your experiments will be the most robust evidence for your stakeholders that you're ready.

Precious time

Sarra Lee, the first person to review the draft of this book, met me though my blog and gave first: she had time between leaving her career at Lloyds Banking Group and starting a new chapter beginning with a Masters in Innovation and offered to help me. I really wanted an objective review before I sent the draft off for its first Development Edit.

Sarra had time to help me. She wouldn't have had time a few years back. With a young family and a pressured job, she didn't have time then to give proper thought to leaving her job, working through the pros and cons.

But she did eventually find time. And she escaped.

Leaving your corporate job might take time for you. You might get to the last page of this book and think 'I'm not ready'.

But one of my favourite words in the English language is 'Yet'.

You may not be ready yet.

Sarra's words are better than mine:

> When I first thought I needed to get out of here I was also mum to a two year old with sleepless nights and nursery fees and a busy and pressured full-time job. I had no idea what I wanted to do and no time to mentally explore.
>
> So it took a few years.
>
> My daughter went to school, started sleeping through and then I could think, hang on, I need to use my mental space to start exploring. I then had more capacity at work to be able to say 'no' or set better boundaries to carve a bit of time out of the day. It takes confidence to even have those difficult conversations so you need to be ready. Timing is everything... but also it is never too late.

Very true, Sarra.

The Escape Plan

This next section is easy. Go to the Escape Plan Canvas in the Appendix and add in your big gaps. The ones that are blocking your exit, your conditions for escape. Only them.

That's it, your Canvas should now be complete.

This is your Escape Plan.

Print it out. Stick it on your wall. Make it real. And now, make it happen.

Ready Player 1?
One of my beta readers, my second Tom Coleman of the book, had a great suggestion at this point, which was to add in a Readiness Checklist, another exercise that would help provide reassurance that you're ready to exit – or identify areas where you still need to do more work, and point you back to the exercises which might help.

So, before you make the leap to Chapter 12, The Great Escape, see how you fare in Exercise 18.

Exercise 18: Readiness Checklist

Exercise instructions

Step 1	Read each question and ask yourself honestly if you recognize any signs that you may not be ready.
Step 2	Give yourself a score out of 10: 1 for a Strong No, 10 for a Strong Yes.
Step 3	Revisit any exercises if you score below a 6.

Chapter summary

o Don't prevaricate with education or training you don't really need.

o Run a series of experiments to find practical ways to close these gaps – if possible before you make the leap.

o If you haven't left your job yet, use the vantage point it brings to experiment risk-free and with the advantages it brings.

o You now have everything you need to build your Escape Plan.

Readiness Checklist

Readiness questions	Signs you may not be ready	Score out of 10	Exercises to revisit
1. Are you clear about why you're leaving?	Inability to articulate top three reasons for leaving. Overly negative about current job and reactive.		1, 4
2. Are you realistic about what life will be like after corporate?	Ignoring realities of instability and uncertainties. Blind faith in grass being greener.		2, 3, 11
3. Have you set goals for your exit?	Avoiding defining what success or failure would look like. Over-confidence that things will turn out ok. Preparing to fail.		13
4. Can you describe your offer and how you add value to others?	Sounding vague, overly self-deprecating or clichéd. Unable to describe what gives you energy or gets you in 'flow'.		5, 6, 7, 8, 12
5. Have you worked up ideas of what you might do next?	Expecting to take some time out to think about what you might do after you've left.		14
6. Have you planned how you will afford life after corporate?	Unwillingness to build a budget, blind faith, over-confidence in sales pipeline.		9
7. Are your most important stakeholders supportive of your move?	Covert operations, planning in stealth-mode, only selling the benefits, shutting down challenge, confirmation bias.		10
8. Do you have a plan to close the gaps which block your exit?	Defining gaps as reasons to stay rather than actions that need to be closed. Unwilling to get specific about actions.		15, 16, 17

CHAPTER 12

The great escape

'How did I escape? With difficulty. How did I plan this moment? With pleasure.'

Alexandre Dumas, The Count of Monte Cristo

The Escape Plan gets you ready. It prepares you for the leap to your brave New World. But it isn't there to hold your hand when you announce your intention to leave to your company, your line managers and your colleagues.

So, I thought I better write something. If only to acknowledge the moment.

My friend Steve was my boss when I told him I wanted to leave and put my name forward for voluntary redundancy. I'd cryptically asked if he would meet me for a walk.

Steve seemed surprised at my decision, which put me off my guard, because I thought he would have guessed. He listened, asked me some thoughtful questions and said OK.

It was something of an anti-climax.

Within 15 minutes we were back talking about the not-very-nice person we worked with.

Then there was the paperwork, the formal submission.

On the day it was due I wobbled a bit when Steve told me which role I was being positioned for in the new organization. I sought support from my coach. As always, she knew exactly what to say: 'Picture yourself in nine months' time. You're in that job. How do you feel?'

'Regretful,' I said, 'That I'd missed a massive opportunity'. I couldn't wait to get off the phone and submit the form.

And once it was approved, I had four months to wait. Four months of gardening leave limbo knowing I was going, kicking my heels, pretending to tidy things up. What a luxury. Four months paid to plan my next move.

But also a weird state.

A few weeks before I left, I was asked to do a short, but high-profile investor relations' project. I was pretty fed up to be honest, to have to do work I was being paid for – I had totally checked out and resented the intrusion.

But eventually I sloped out under the cover of lockdown.

Not everyone's exit is quite so graceful.

Think Lehman Brothers' staff walking out with their boxes with the media snapping away. Or indeed anyone who doesn't really want to leave.

Good practices

Regardless of whether you leave quietly as I did or with the shock and awe of Lehman's, there are some good practices you can try to follow when exiting:

1. Have a plan
It's kind of late in the book if you're just getting this point.

Most people resign once they have something else to join. They serve out their notice in one organization, and, if they're lucky, they get a nice break for a holiday and join another.

That's probably the right model too when leaving corporate life.

Know where you're going.

Not only is this much better for your ego, which can become quite bruised by leaving (voluntarily and especially under duress), but it is also good for maintaining networks.

People like to know that we're going to be alright – and they might even want to keep in touch. It's awkward for everyone if we're wailing. Or flailing.

Even if you haven't got a plan, make one up. It might end up becoming what you do.

I'm not a fan of the vague 'I'm going to take some time out to think about what I want'. It's the corporate equivalent of falling off the planet.

2. Take what you can
Obviously don't steal, but there are things that are fair game. Like your annual reviews, internal CVs, training information – you will forget what you've done. HR records, copies of payslips, share options. Any personal stuff on your laptop, photos or documents. Bookmarks to external information you might struggle to find again.

Pretty much everything you did for the company is owned by the company so don't take any of that, but you can write a list for yourself of what you created or were involved in.

I found it hard to project forward enough so there were things I realized I'd left on my computer or not asked someone about, which became problematic later. No matter how good your relations were with colleagues before you left, a wall goes up after you leave when it comes to sharing.

3. Maintain your networks
Before I left, I did copy a load of email addresses of people I thought might become useful. Most haven't to be honest. But there were others who I hadn't expected to become useful,

whose email addresses I had to guess. So, give this some thought before you go.

Talk to people before you leave, tell them what you're doing, get them excited for you and where appropriate, plan to meet up when the dust settles – somewhere neutral. People don't change wanting to help other people. They're just awkward because they're staying and you're not. The more you can do to reduce the awkwardness, the more likely you'll shorten the gap to see them again (if that's what you want).

Your company may have an alumni network or LinkedIn group for leavers. But I recommend forming your own and activating it yourself.

In fact, my community were the early readers of the Corporate Escapologist blog, which led me to write this book. Many were my beta-readers, my podcast guests and have become really good friends.

4. Leave positively
No matter how much your blood is boiling or if you feel like crying, maintain a positive demeanour. Fake it if you must. No-one wants to see someone losing control, it doesn't help anyone – least of all you. So, keep the ranting and the tears for a closed circle and never show them in the office.

Mainly because you will get over it – but this may be the enduring memory people have of you. And you really don't want that.

5. Exhaust any benefits
There are some benefits you should sort before you leave, because they're either easier or cheaper than organizing them yourselves. My company had a whole load of benefits with other organizations you could access, like subscriptions to Headspace, Cycle to Work, insurances, health schemes, etc.

An hour surfing the company intranet might be a good use of your time. But make sure not to sign up for things that could be cheaper after you've left. It will come as no surprise to learn that corporates overpay for a lot of things you can buy cheaper in the real world, so you might be better waiting.

Outplacement

You might be offered some Outplacement or Transition Services as part of your exit. Corporates offer them to help you through the process of leaving to prepare for what's next.

A bit like this book. Except not.

These services mostly work for people who want to get a similar job to the one they've left. They help with CV writing, LinkedIn profiles, job searches and interview techniques. All pretty worthy, but only if you're looking to jump to another corporate.

They won't help you explore a wide range of opportunities, experiment with a few, run portfolio careers or even start your own business. They can't help here.

Mainly because they're measured on getting people into jobs as quickly as possible to assuage any lingering corporate guilt about the redundancies.

I'm working with a few of the more enlightened outplacement firms that recognize the gap in their offer and are more open to providing alternative services.

If you get outplacement support from your company, I hope it helps you. It's a people-based business, so if you get a good person to help, you may get somewhere.

But I've written this book so you needn't be disappointed if you don't.

Fading out

As much as I like the idea of storming out from a job in a blaze of glory, the truth is you will probably fade out. You stop getting invited to meetings about next year or a new project on the horizon. You find new Microsoft SharePoints you can't access. Spreadsheets circulate but your name is missing.

You might feel a twinge of sadness, rejection, declining status – maybe even regret.

And that's perfectly normal. But you might also be feeling more than a twinge of relief, optimism, even excitement.

Especially about having escaped that SharePoint.

Leaving dos

I left in lockdown so there was no party for me. Leaving was pretty anti-climactic. My final Teams call and a courier came to collect my laptop.

I was, however, hugely relieved to avoid a leaving do.

But you may want one – or need one. It may be part of your processing. Like a funeral. It may be recognition you need for the work you've done, the relationships you've made, the impact you've had. You may deserve one.

If so, enjoy it. Be humble and grateful if asked to say a few words. Don't drink too much, say too much or gloat too much.

If you want one, make it before you leave; if it comes afterwards, everyone's moved on, including you, and it's forced, with a thinner crowd (but maybe that's a good thing – just the diehards).

The leaving do may present an opportunity to practise your new identity. Few may understand it and that's fine – they're not your customer or your new tribe of supporters. But give them an answer rather than crumple under mild interrogation – and, you never know, it may lead to something.

Your final day

When it comes to your final day, walk out the door, or more probably click 'Leave' on your final Teams call, and hold your head up high. If you want to have a bit of a cry or alternatively jump for joy, both are perfectly acceptable responses to have in private.

But do celebrate it.

Go out for dinner, open a nice bottle of wine and toast your corporate experience and all you've gained. Because you should feel grateful for the opportunity you've had – even if it wasn't always what you'd expected.

And moreover, you should feel optimistic because everything you've learnt is now going to be packaged up into something that makes you even happier, fulfilled and free.

Chapter summary

o Leave well.

o Prepare for leaving – don't leave anything on the table you might need later.

o Make any outplacement or transition services work for you.

o Don't get drunk at your leaving do.

o Celebrate leaving.

V Sustain your exit

You made it to the other side – well done! I hope you feel proud of yourself.

You should, because most people don't see the exit through. They never get that far. They teeter on the edge and decide it looks too scary and retreat. You are amongst the happy minority who have backed yourself.

And now you're going to win.

You have invested in the work to maximize your chances of success.

You have done the hard part, the truly brave part. But there is another hard part ahead that will continue to test you – and that is sustaining this life.

Staying escaped.

Part V of the Escape Method deals with the reality that your trajectory over the next few years is unlikely to be a straight line. It is very likely to go down as well as up (sometimes both in one day) and you are likely to wobble over your decision.

You will be tempted to give up everything for which you've worked.

Think of those reality shows where 'ordinary' people join the SAS for a couple of months or swim under ice in the Arctic. They're really testing themselves.

And this will test you.

You might even decide to go back. And that's ok. Just make sure you're actively choosing it – not settling for it.

I will end this part of the book by helping you to channel your inner (annoying) child by asking 'Are we there yet?'

CHAPTER 13

No straight lines

'*Beginnings are always messy*'.

John Galsworthy, Author

If there's one word that characterizes life in the 2020s it's 'fluid'. I think it's a beautiful word, full of opportunities, open minds, choices, with barriers broken down. Multiple ways to live our lives.

Our need for fluidity has been trending since at least the 1960s – but in recent years things have undoubtedly accelerated.

You have choice. And the right to change your mind. And fail.

It's like you can't really be wrong. Everything is an experiment anyway.

Try to enjoy this period and don't be too hard on yourself if everything doesn't go neatly to plan.

And it may not.

The early days

After the initial euphoria of exiting wears off, you can be left with a nasty hangover.

It can be lonely. You may have too much time. The phone may not ring. There's tumbleweed on your socials. You know you're just doing busy work. And taking ages over it – perfecting everything à la corporate.

Without structure, you've got to build your own. That might be establishing a new working rhythm. For instance, I try not to work Fridays.

This gives me a day every week when I appreciate not having my corporate job. And it also gives me only four days to get everything else done.

You might sit somewhere specific in your house – I nearly always sit at my office desk with the door shut, to signal both to myself and my family that 'I am working (do not disturb)'. I put an hour in my calendar for lunch each day with my wife. It doesn't always happen, but without the reminder, I suspect it never would.

To begin with I was religious about using Trello, the Kanban board you can get online or download as an app. At first I added in a few tasks I wanted to complete, then I started colour coding them with different themes, like the consulting gigs, my startup, the blog. Over time, a backlog emerged with things I wanted to get to if I had time.

What it did for me was provide a daily and weekly focus. Each Thursday night I planned what I wanted to deliver by the following Thursday. I tried very hard not to do anything that wasn't on the list, but I wasn't obsessive. What Trello also did was give me a sense of how productive I had been each week – did I do what I had planned?

I didn't go through the whole effort of holding a retrospective with myself to see what worked well, less well and what needed to change… but it did influence how I planned my work the following week.

For a while Trello was my best friend, reassuring me that I was making progress and nudging me when I was off beam.

I know other people go for a walk each day, make coffee at the same time, do the school runs, shop on particular days. There were a couple of people I had regular calls with; people who were going through something similar. Whatever works for you.

You'll change your routines over time, based on how your new life shakes out. But to begin with a basic structure can help avoid the temptation to turn on daytime TV, doomscroll for hours – or in my case weed the garden (my own Forth Bridge).

I think the other thing is to try to manage your expectations. Which means lower them.

If you had simply flipped from one corporate job to another you would feel, and probably be, pretty useless for a few months, maybe longer. It's just the same here. An adjustment. Lean into it. It's part of your transition, finding what works for you. Don't be too hard on yourself.

In my early days I used to hear from lots of people finding this period tough. Some were dealing with a form of grief from not feeling needed or relevant. Others were feeling rudderless. Their experience fuelled my blog because I knew this period was so challenging.

I hope reading this book has helped start you off before you made the leap, so you're not kicking off day 1 with a blank sheet of paper, 'Now what shall I do with my next 25 years?' Terrifying.

Look back at the gaps in your Escape Plan. I'd eat my proverbial hat if you had ticked off each one of those activities before you exited. So start there.

Who cares if it's a bit of 'busy work' in the early days?

Find your rhythm, find your focus, find what works for you.

Virtue in messy

This messy phase can feel quite uncomfortable for corporate types used to structure, process and order. But like many new things, it can actually be pretty good for you. It's a much more creative space to be starting out in, where you're likely to stretch into different places, meet different people, seize opportunities.

One fellow Corporate Escapologist, Karin, who left corporate life years ago to set up her own digital marketing consultancy, told me she felt like there was 'a whole universe of serendipity opening up' as she left. In her old company her network and the opportunities in it were constrained, but released into a bigger pond, the opportunities increased.

But serendipity can be messy – and unreliable. And like the dating metaphor, you've got to kiss a lot of frogs before you find your prince or princess. It can be inefficient and, at times, quite painful. One step forward, ten steps back.

Before you know, it you're back on the veranda (from Chapter 4).

And you won't like it. It will feel like failing. And that wasn't really allowed in our corporate jobs. One step back maybe. But two you'd probably find yourself replaced.

This messy phase is likely to be a major adjustment.

But do embrace it, because it's often in uncertainty, ambiguity and fluidity that interesting things can happen.

My world at BP was pretty insular; the people I met were like everyone else I met – and they were mostly terrific, bright, interesting people. But after a while I'd met everyone I needed to know to get my job done and I rarely met anyone new.

Compared with when I left, I talked to strangers. Not in a weird way. In a curious way. Without an agenda. Or an outcome. Sometimes it didn't even need to be planned ('Are you free now?'). Fewer rules and formats.

Just conversations. Lots of them. And they were fascinating. Listening and learning and sharing and laughing and making connections and comparing and contrasting.

And they led to more conversations. And job offers, proposals, Come-and-join-my-startups, You-should-speak-tos, and Read-this, Go-here, Watch-this.

My mind exploded, my opportunities increased, my self-confidence built.

I became good at doing things I'd always told myself I was bad at: small talk, networking, talking to strangers.

And I even got better at doing them in front of more than one person. I spoke on podcasts, joined Instagram Lives, participated in other people's workshops, became a guest speaker at fireside chats.

Messy can lead to opportunity.

And to diversity in the people I met, the ideas I began to have and the new things I experienced – and it made me feel more confident.

My life feels richer today because of these connections in my life.

It's an unexpected benefit of leaving a great company to build something great for myself.

Wobbles, I've had a few

I'm only human. So are you. And there will be times when you will wobble.

If you're looking for smooth sailing, you probably should have stayed in your corporate job. Should I have mentioned that earlier? Come on, you haven't got this far through the book because you're a continuous improvement kind of character.

You may wake at 3am wondering what the heck you've done. And because it's 3am not 3pm, you won't be entirely rational or balanced. You won't be distracted by a phone call, a school run or an Amazon delivery. So you can really slide headlong into a vortex of misery.

I recommend planning for it. Assume it will happen and get prepared – with chocolate by the bedside.

In my experience there are five broad areas where you're likely to wobble. The trick is to prepare some simple logic in advance to face-off the demons so you can go back to whatever you were doing. More often than not it will have been sleeping.

1   **Finances**: I hate it being the first, but I feel naïve pretending it's not the most important factor for most of us. It may not be for you, but if it is, you need to work out how you're

going to afford your new life. Part of your preparation may have been to build a back-up fund or buffer, or secure some contract work, or something part-time. You may have found a way to make money from a side-hustle without even leaving. Or you might have got lucky with a pay-off. It may take time to find the way to calm your 3am panic around the financials – for me it was having a buffer and a robust budget, both took me a year I'd say.

2   **Why**: you'll definitely question whether it was really worth leaving your safe corporate job for this life of uncertainty. Many, many times. You're on the veranda again. In the early days, you may not have seen the benefits, so it can be hard to bat the question away. But over time you will. For me, I have this North Star of how I want to work (autonomy, variety and pace – as well as feeling more connected to my family). Even if I'm struggling with things like the finances or projects not coming off when I expect, recalling my North Star can ground me and stop me spiralling. What would do the same for you?

3   **Buy-in**: Not having the support of an important stakeholder can really keep you up all night worrying. Firstly, you need facts not fears here – make sure your concerns are valid and not just 'in your head'. If you wake up worrying what your partner or parent or a client thinks, talk to them the next day. Try to understand what's really important to them. Involve them in how you're feeling and the decisions you're making – often that can be enough.

4   **Options**: One of my wobbles, which I could have foreseen, given my butterfly mind, was carrying too many options – and not really committing to any. Waking up at 3am, I used to cycle through them one after another – feeling bad they weren't progressing. Writing things down can really help. In my experience, as soon as you start applying some detail and description, the flaky options fade. You need to be able to write your options down with minimal arm-waving, and ideally with some evidence that they aren't based on some elaborate Ponzi scheme. For other people the 3am worry might be too few options – all your eggs in one basket. To deal with these wobbles, go back to Part III and think more

deeply about what other Corporate Escapologists are doing and brainstorm some ideas that play to your strengths, skills and experience.

5 **Gaps**: There will be things you can't do well (yet) – and you can easily fixate on them when you're feeling vulnerable. They can be enough to stop you exiting in the first place. I can't count the number of hours I've lost sleep worrying about how poor I am at sales (to wake up the following morning and remember I'm actually *good enough* at it – and I'm not expecting to make a career out of it). Again, having some rational fob-offs to hand can really dispel the gloom and reverse the Bad Thinking. Make sure all those gaps in your Escape Plan have an action to close them and you should be able to snuggle down and get some shut-eye.

Teetering on the precipice is a horrible feeling. Even if it's all in your head.

The wobbles can attack during the daytime too.

Many people talk about getting sucked into looking for jobs on LinkedIn – or their former company's career site. I like to say 'many people' as if that wasn't me. Several times I applied for jobs that were not worthy of my skills and experience because I wanted to escape the uncertainty. And I *didn't even get an interview*. Once I even emailed the hiring manager of a job in BP, looking for a leg-up. She didn't even respond.

The wobbles don't last long. Especially, if you have properly prepared to leave – beginning by understanding why you want to leave. That North Star from Chapter 7 gives you a floor, below which the rational you knows you can't fall.

For instance, if working remotely is an explicit goal for your new life and a tempting job proposal comes your way, if it's office-based five days a week, it's simple, you can't go for it. It's incompatible with something much bigger than your need for certainty. Same, if you are, like me, looking for autonomy – it's stopped me multiple times investigating job opportunities.

And once I'm through the wobbles, I am ALWAYS relieved that nothing happened. Including not getting the job offers. Because I don't want to waste my time with interviews and application forms, learning some other blend of politics, going to pointless meetings, etc. etc.

And neither will you.

It's a bit like a hangover. It'll pass. Feel sorry for yourself a bit, eat some carbs and then as you hit rock bottom and start to turn a corner, accelerate and move towards the light.

You've got this.

Because it's what you want.

Staying in touch

After six months or so I did some consultancy for BP. Only once. It wasn't a good experience being on the other side.

You might have planned ongoing work as part of your Escape Plan, which is fine. But don't think it will be the same. You're not the same, nor are they. You left. You're no longer part of the family – or the furniture.

Which is what you wanted, isn't it?

My experience, when catching up with people who haven't left, is that conversations can quickly become quite negative: 'Nothing's changed', 'It's even worse', 'You were lucky you got out when you did'.

It's tempting to stir the pot, but don't.

You will also notice that people want to catch up with you when they're thinking of leaving. They look on you somewhat heroically and want to know the formula. Obviously you can now point them to this book.

But while you will want to help, most won't leave – they are looking to vent with someone who feels like you felt (note the past tense). Be selective how you spend your time – it's now more precious than theirs.

You don't need my permission to stay in touch with people from your old job, especially if you were genuine out-of-work friends but remember you've got a whole world to explore.

You're off that veranda now, don't waste time looking back.

Chapter summary

o   The early days will feel strange – expect it and you won't be disappointed.

o   You have to make stuff happen yourself – that's the biggest difference now. It's all on you, but that is also exciting and liberating.

o   Manage the wobbles by going back to why you wanted this change of life and your goals.

o   Be wary of staying in touch with your old company and manage your expectations.

CHAPTER 14

Going back

'It is impossible to live without failing at something unless you live so cautiously that you might as well not have lived at all, in which case you have failed by default.'

JK Rowling, Author

This will be a short chapter. The shortest in fact.

I'm not really interested in going back and I'm not sure you should be either.

Unless you've found it hard to meet your financial goals, which can happen, you are unlikely to find fulfilment by going back.

Never say never. And I've certainly been tempted to join other corporates.

But if I went back, I know I would trade things I deeply value today (autonomy, variety, pace) for things I value less (predictable salary, status, not having to explain my job to strangers).

And it would feel like – maybe it would be – a backward step.

But that's me. You're different.

And you might have very sound, logical reasons to go back.

I have, however, in writing this book, tried to think more rationally about going back. Three things have struck me:

1   If I did go back, I couldn't work as long again for one
    company, I'd be too old (just).

2   If I did go back, I'd never have the same lock-in as I had
    with pension, redundancy, benefits – they will never be as
    good again.

3   Because of 1 and 2, I would never feel so incentivized to
    stay as long and so I could go join a corporate for a couple
    of years – and then step out again.

I could become a corporate boomerang, something another
friend of mine, John, has become, flipping back and forth
multiple times to fit with his love of travel and his passion for
photography.

And he's not alone.

Effie's story

Effie worked 12 years for major corporates, Skype, Marks &
Spencer and HP, delivering transformational programmes,
but at heart she is an entrepreneur. Alongside her corporate
job, Effie built an e-commerce side-hustle before anyone knew
what that meant. Eventually, she left corporate life, even
securing funding from Deborah Meaden on Dragons' Den.

Over time, Effie moved on from her startup and went back into
corporate life – first contracting and then setting up her own
marketing agencies to offer services to corporate clients.

Over the years, Effie has moved between a series of salaried
jobs, freelance and startups – as she told me, 'I've seen going
back into corporates as a way to learn new skills, build new
networks and see problems I think I can fix. Then I see
opportunities to leave and want to go it alone'.

Effie built a 10,000-strong community of makers on Instagram
called the Handmade Association, where she runs online
coaching and classes to help creatives build businesses. For
the past few years, Effie has been building Boost, a fractional
marketing agency, that provides experienced marketing
professionals to support medium-sized companies who want

quality marketing talent without the cost of taking on full-time staff. Right now she's creating opportunities for more Corporate Escapologists. But she hasn't written off the idea of ever going back to a corporate job – for the right reasons.

You can find Effie on LinkedIn (search: Effie Moss) or visit Boost at weareboostagency.com.

Be intentional
Going back to corporate is as much a personal decision as leaving in the first place.

It's all about being intentional, going back because it's the right thing for you.

But if you're thinking of accepting a job that takes you back to corporate life, ask yourself these questions:

1   Why am I taking this job? Am I scared of something or am I positively choosing it?

2   How will I satisfy the needs and benefits I have appreciated in my new life in a corporate job?

3   How will I feel about this decision in six months?

4   Will my financial situation really improve?

5   Is there any other way I could take the job while retaining some of what I have today?

6   How will I feel if I say no?

Make sure you want to move back for the right reasons; positive reasons that will give you joy, fulfilment and make you proud of yourself.

Lecture over.

CHAPTER 15

How will you know you're there?

'If you want to be happy, be'.

Leo Tolstoy, Writer

Is the grass really greener? Good question, I'm really glad you asked.

The answer is 'It depends'. On the day you're asking it. Sometimes even the time of day you're asking it.

Generally speaking, for me it's a firm yes – and for most people I know it's that way too. Once Pandora's Box is opened to autonomy, flexibility, variety and a load of other things that really make you feel good, it's hard to close it.

'Are we there yet?'

It's one of those annoying questions children ask on long journeys. The reason it drives us up the wall is because it's blinking obvious we are not there – otherwise we would have stopped the car and got out. That kind of journey has a defined end-state, whereas yours may not. You may never be 'there' yet.

You may be comfortable with this, in which case great – you can move on, there's nothing to see here.

But maybe you're reading this chapter pre-leap, or mid-leap. You're wondering how you can expect to feel – and whether this will measure up.

You need something objective that validates your decision to exit corporate life so you can get on with living your new life.

Test it

It's good to have some tests you can run periodically or when you're in need of a reminder (e.g. at 3am) about why you're doing this, what you're gaining – and why it matters.

Exercise 19 provides three 'Made It' tests... linked to the work you did earlier in the book, that set out why you left in the first place and what you hoped you'd get out of leaving.

Exercise 19: Three 'Made It' Tests

Exercise instructions

Step 1	This one is easy. It's a tick and bash exercise. Ask yourself these questions honestly.

Give yourself a couple of months before running these tests. They're supposed to be a reasonably high bar that you set before you left and not a walk in the park.

Aiming to pass them within a few weeks implies they weren't demanding enough. Or maybe you were so ready to leave you'd mentally left long, long ago.

Analyzing your scores

Mostly ticks – you're on your way to having escaped and moved on. The Escape Plan worked or at least it got you in the right state to exit. Don't spend lots of time over-analyzing why you couldn't give each test a clean sweep, good enough is good enough. Unless you want to explore. But perfection involves too much unnecessary overthinking. I'd say 75% is good enough.

Three 'Made It' Tests

Purpose test	Y/N	Resilience test	Y/N	Financial test	Y/N
1. Am I working in the way I hoped?		**1.** Do I belive I can create value outside?		**1.** Am I worrying about money every day?	
2. Am I achieving more balance?		**2.** Have I a broad enough offer that plays to my strengths?		**2.** Have I built a buffer?	
3. Do I feel in control?		**3.** Have I got options if things don't go my way?		**3.** Am I using a budget?	
4. Am I proud of myself?		**4.** Am I feeling more resilient?		**4.** Can I see a way to replace the income I used to make?	
5. Do I feel more in 'flow' than I did?		**5.** Have I got the right new identity?		**5.** If something changes do I have options?	

Halfy-halfy – there may be some things you still need to work on if you want to stay escaped – and stop the wandering eye on LinkedIn. Right now, you're not getting as many of the benefits you expected from the escape. Were you realistic or is something not working? What do you need to do more of or less of? If it's on the reward side of things, are you expecting too much, too soon? Do you need to be more patient?

Mostly crosses – ok, Houston we have a problem. It doesn't feel like it's working. Yet. Assuming you haven't run the test in week two, maybe you need to go back to some fundamentals.

If you've left and still think leaving is the right thing for you, drop me a line at adam@corporateescapology.com. I think your situation is frankly so unusual there must be something I can do to help. Either you need to set your goals and aspirations closer to reality – or you need some help to get you going. Either way I am here for you.

Have a little patience

'To lose patience is to lose the battle.'

Mahatma Gandhi.

Easy said Mahatma.

It takes time to feel stable. Most people agree it's a couple of years. Hardly rapid response I know. For someone deeply impatient, that's tough – and tougher still, if those around you long for a return to the stability of the old days. But patient you must be.

Your corporate career was years in the making, from school onwards, so it's only fair to allow some time to get your new life right now. Corporate people are conditioned to optimize – they create order, they join dots, they stabilize. And for a long time it may feel too rocky to even think about optimizing.

But make sure you don't sabotage your exit by saying 'this isn't working' too early on.

Productivity author Mike Sturm talks about the 'Tragedy of the forward-progress bias' where because something appears not to be working or moving us forward, we claim failure: 'we tend to see anything that's not clearly forward progress as a setback. In other words: We think If we're not gaining ground, we're losing it.'

It's not true of course, because it's often in the failures that we learn the things that accelerate our progress later on. And you may be succeeding in lots of areas, but fixating on the few things that are going less well.

Talking to people who have made it through to their other side, they describe a very gradual transition to becoming comfortable.

Arnab, who we met in Chapter 9, said after a year and a half, his coach observed that their sessions had shifted from 'obsessing about his exit and were now focused on the future'. Katie, author and consultant, told me that after a couple of years she booked a three-week holiday and 'I realised that I'd never been able to afford that – time or money – when I was in my old job. That was a key moment for me'. Or as another Corporate Escapologist, Binu, told me, 'I just stopped comparing this life to my old life – it was like the old life couldn't compare, so I didn't try'.

For me I noticed after a couple of years that things just felt stable. I'd stopped worrying about money and I stopped thinking that this might (have to) end.

It felt like this was my life.

I'd normalized it.

Whatever path you choose, whatever stage you're at, I hope you're starting to feel happier with the decision you've taken.

It's brave to change. As the writer Anaïs Nin wrote in *Mirages: The Unexpurgated Diary of Anaïs Nin, 1939–1947*: 'Life shrinks or expands in proportion to one's courage.'

Now your life is expanding, be courageous.

Chapter summary

o   Feeling stable takes time, maybe several years.

o   Be kind to yourself.

o   Use your goals to build data and objectivity around how you're feeling.

o   Have patience, good things take time to mature.

Final thoughts

'I can't leave'. That's what Rhiannon said to me during our first call. 'I hate it but I have to stay, I don't even know what I'd do'. And the bit that really got to me: 'I don't know who would want me.'

Rhiannon (not her real name) is a married woman in her mid-40s, with two teenage children. She has two degrees, she's mid-level at work, gets good performance reviews, works well with people, is bright, funny and extremely reliable.

But her self-confidence was at rock bottom. She told me she felt trapped because she needed the job, but the thought of having to do it for 20 more years made her want to run for the hills. The word that kept going through my mind was 'desolate'. It's such an evocative word, hopeless, bereft of options and lonely, but it's all I could think about.

Rhiannon was not ready to leave her corporate job. She needed it. Partly for the practical reasons of income and partly because she needed the stability it afforded, to give her time to plan her escape.

And as much as she didn't want to hear it, it would take her a year or more to leave safely and successfully.

It nearly sent her over the edge when I said this, because she'd heard I'd helped people leave in a month or two. And I have. But not people in this state.

The good news for Rhiannon was that as she began to prepare, she would feel better about herself and her job, more resilient, stronger and more confident. She was at rock bottom, but she wouldn't be for long.

I wrote *Corporate Escapology* for people like Rhiannon. And for the millions more who know there's more to life than the daily grind, people who know they've settled and their corporate job no longer serves them – people who want change but fear change.

Life is short and it's full of opportunities. So it's doubly absurd we stay doing things that don't fulfil us, don't help us grow, don't make us happy.

I started this book talking about how our relationship with work has changed over the decades – and particularly over the years since the pandemic. And this is the context for people like us expecting more: more from our jobs, more from our employers, more from ourselves.

We expect change yet we're often doing the same thing on repeat. Like Einstein's definition of insanity.

The time passes. New distractions, a pat on the head, a bonus. And suddenly we're back in the game.

But not the right game. Because those artificial sweeteners don't last very long. And in my experience they start to leave a bad aftertaste. Before too long it's all you notice.

The taste is bad enough, but it's what it does to our self-confidence, self-belief and self-worth that made me write this book.

The mission of *Corporate Escapology* is to inspire and build confidence.

We owe a great deal to our corporate careers and what we have been able to learn, experience, practise, observe and master over the years we've been employed. Our corporate careers have been formative, they've made us who we are.

We should celebrate them.

But we don't owe them anything; we added enough value when we were there.

It's now your time to break free and move on.

You can escape.

Leap.

And land safely and successfully my friend.

Appendix
Escape Plan Canvas

Things I want in my new life

Realities I can't avoid

Motivations for change

Stakeholders I need to consider

Fears holding me back

Boundaries I need to respect

SEKSE

Ideas I want to explore

Possible new identities

OKRs

Gaps

Further reading

Nothing makes me appreciate the two parts of my brain like reading. The right side wants to be transported to new worlds, lives and times with novels like *The Count of Monte Cristo*, *The Forsyte Saga* and *Jack Reacher* (judge away). And my left side wants to learn things, methods, techniques, what works.

Corporate Escapology has been a few years in the making and these books have been some of its high-quality ingredients.

The Squiggly Career, Helen Tupper and Sarah Ellis, Portfolio Penguin (2020) – a good tool to start thinking outside your corporate cube, to seeing the bigger you.

The Multi-Hyphen Method, Emma Gannon, Hodder & Stoughton (2018) – a celebration of the portfolio career, how technology has enabled us to be so much more than a one trick corporate pony.

The Success Myth, Emma Gannon, Transworld Digital (2023) – a reality check on what success means in this modern, slightly crazy, world.

Revolting Women, Lucy Ryan, Practical Inspiration Publishing (2023) – a rallying cry to dismantle the entrenched sexism and ageism that prevents more experienced women from delivering on their potential.

224 | Further reading

The Power of Regret, Dan Pink, Canongate Books (2022) – a new way to look at regret as a force to help us become better people, to make better decisions – and how to use regret to our advantage.

Range: How Generalists Triumph in a Specialized World, David Epstein, Macmillan (2019) – a book to make those of us who can do many things well (enough) feel better about ourselves; a book that shows us we're more relevant in today's world of rapidly changing, wicked problems.

The Song of Significance, Seth Godin, Penguin Business (2023) – a call for more meaning, more connection and more humanity as a way of avoiding the race-to-the-bottom, robots-will-rule-the-world dystopic vision.

Atomic Habits, James Clear, Random House Business (2018) – a book that teaches us that sustainable progress is the sum of many little things done each day, rather than crazy pivots and nonsense transformations that don't stick.

Daring Greatly: How the Courage to Be Vulnerable Transforms the Way We Live, Love, Parent, and Lead, Brené Brown, Penguin Life (2015) – a plea to open up, to be more honest, to be flawed as a way to connect and to feel life, not just observe it.

Thinking Fast and Slow, Daniel Kahneman, Penguin (2012) – a wise treatise that gives us the tools to enable us to observe ourselves, question ourselves and improve ourselves.

Designing your Life, Bill Burnett, Dave Evans, Vintage (2017) – a method for building the life you want.

On a Friday: Make a Difference/a Handbook for Leaders, Like Hearted Leaders (2022) – a compilation of lovely stories by some lovely leaders.

Escaping corporate life will invariably lead to you building a business of sorts. Here are some of the best books that have helped me:

For teaching me to start small, cheap and test everything: **Lean Startup, Eric Ries**, Portfolio Penguin (2011).

For teaching me to get out and talk to customers: **Four Steps to the Epiphany, Steve Blank**, Wiley (2020).

For teaching me that only my customer is right when it comes to my brilliant business ideas: **The Mom Test, Rob Fitzpatrick**, CreateSpace Independent Publishing Platform (2013).

For teaching me really practical steps to understand my customer: **Do Penguins Eat Peaches, Katie Tucker**, Practical Inspiration Publishing (2023).

For teaching me the concept of exponential value for less effort: **Turning the Flywheel, Jim Collins**, Random House Business (2019).

For teaching me everything that's worth knowing about marketing and customers: **This is Marketing, Seth Godin**, Portfolio Penguin (2018).

For teaching me the importance of engaging people with stories: **The Science of Storytelling, Will Storr**, William Collins (2020).

For teaching me different ways of testing my ideas with real customers: **Testing Business Ideas: A Field Guide for Rapid Experimentation, David Bland**, Alexander Osterwalder, Wiley (2019).

For teaching me everything I need to know about PR: **Hype Yourself, Lucy Werner**, Practical Inspiration Publishing (2020).

Acknowledgements

To Megan for always believing in me. I thank my lucky stars every day you chose to live your life with me.

To Tilly, Ella and Bertie, I'm so very proud of each one of you and grateful for you. You give me purpose.

To the remaining Forbes family, we each have different memories of Mum, but we can all agree she spent a lot of time in bed reading. I know she'd be so proud of us all – and of Dad for managing so well without her.

To my incredible Beta Readers: Sarra, Miffa, Nicole, Jade, Tom and Katie. I will never forget your generosity of time and honesty – you have made this book so much better, thank you.

To Claire for your lovely Foreword and for sharing your story on my podcast. It still makes me laugh that your Dad's still hoping you'll go back to the Law!

To Paul for taking the Corporate Escapologist out of my head and on to paper. Your drawings elevate this book and make it truly special. You can find Paul's work at tavenerdesign.uk.

To the people who have let me tell their stories of escaping corporate life: Katie, Steve, Chris, Niall, David, Martin, Tom, Charlie, Erica, Claire, Kia, Lilli, Effie, Stephanie, Christy, Dayna, Devi and a few others who prefer to remain anonymous. You are the brave ones who will now inspire bravery in others.

To Miffa, my coach and friend, who challenges me, counsels me and champions me. I wouldn't have written this book without you. You made me believe I had something worthwhile to say and that I was the person to say it.

Three men (but thankfully no baby) were pivotal in my transition from Corporate Lifer to Corporate Escapologist: Philipp, John and Illai. Your belief in me changed how I began to see myself. Without you three I might never have escaped and this book would never have been written. I'm enormously proud to call each one of you my friend.

And lastly, to everyone at Practical Inspiration Publishing who turned my words and Paul's pictures into a real life book. Alison, you are a very special publisher – I owe Katie for helping me find you.

The final acknowledgement is to you, dear Reader, for investing your time in this book and for trusting me to help. I hope you now feel ready to begin a new and exciting chapter of your life.

About the author

Adam Forbes escaped a full-time corporate career to build a life with more family, fulfilment and fun. He now coaches others using the Escape Method described in this book. Adam is on a mission to help people recognize their true value, build their self-confidence and change their lives for the better using the amazing skills, experience and know-how developed during their corporate careers.

You can find Adam on Instagram @corporateescapologist, on LinkedIn and on Substack where he writes a weekly blog as the Corporate Escapologist. You can find out more about Adam's coaching and workshops at corporateescapology.com.

Index

Printed in the USA
CPSIA information can be obtained
at www.ICGtesting.com
JSHW071339080724
66043JS00007B/54

9 781788 606028